Mammoth Science

Mammoth Science

(with a little help from some elephant shrews)

David Macaulay

Senior Editor Jenny Sich
Senior Art Editor Stefan Podhorodecki
Editors Kelsie Besaw, Vicky Richards
US Editor Megan Douglass
Designer Kit Lane
Jacket Design Development Manager
Sophia MTT
Jacket Designers Stefan Podhorodecki,
Priyanka Bansal
Senior DTP Designer Harish Aggarwal
Production Editor Rob Dunn
Production Controller Sian Cheung
Managing Editor Francesca Baines
Managing Art Editor Philip Letsu
Publisher Andrew Macintyre
Art Director Karen Self
Associate Publishing Director Liz Wheeler
Publishing Director Jonathan Metcalf

Contributors Jack Challoner,
Andrea Mills, Georgia Mills
Consultants Derek Harvey, Penny Johnson

With thanks to Helen Peters for the index and
Victoria Pyke for proofreading

First American Edition, 2020
Published in the United States by DK Publishing
1450 Broadway, Suite 801, New York, NY 10018

A catalog record for this book
is available from the Library of Congress.
ISBN: 978–1–4654–9146–6

Printed and bound in Canada

FOR THE CURIOUS
www.dk.com

Contents

Matter

States of matter

Everything around you is made of matter. From trees to computers to the air you're breathing—if it takes up space, it's matter. Matter exists in three main states: solid, liquid, and gas. When a substance changes from one state to another, it is still made up of exactly the same tiny particles. But the particles behave in very different ways in each state, as demonstrated by the mammoths in these three beakers.

Floating free
Real gases (not made of mammoths) are usually much harder to see.

Solid
In this beaker, the mammoth matter is forming a solid. The particles are locked together in a strong, dense structure and don't want to let go of each other. This is why solids have a fixed shape.

Solids keep their shape

Liquid
Here, the mammoth matter is a liquid. The particles are still closely packed, but they can slide over each other. They flow to take the shape of the container.

Mammoth matter
The mammoths represent the tiny particles that make up matter. The particles in this mammoth matter stay the same, but the way they behave changes dramatically from state to state.

Gas

As a gas, the mammoth matter can't be contained by an open beaker. The particles are not bonded together and whiz about freely to take up any available space.

Ice
At temperatures lower than 32°F (0°C) water freezes solid. Its particles lose energy and become locked together in a fixed shape. Water is unusual because it expands as it freezes, taking up more space. This means ice is less dense than water, which is why ice floats.

Frozen solid
Encased in ice, this mammoth is having a chilling experience.

Thawing out
Drip by drip, the mammoth emerges as the ice melts.

Changing states

Most substances can change state—from solid to liquid to gas and back again. You can make a substance change its state by changing its temperature. Heating a solid substance gives its particles more energy so they move around more and can melt into a liquid, then evaporate into a gas. Cooling a gas makes it condense into a liquid and then freeze solid.

Ice, water, vapor
Water is the only substance on Earth that occurs naturally in all three states of matter: as solid ice, liquid water, and gaseous water vapor. Luckily for this frozen mammoth, it's not too difficult to make water change from state to state— you just have to turn up the heat.

State to state

Water can change back and forth between its states endlessly. Ice melts into water, which evaporates into steam, and steam condenses into water, which freezes into ice. Usually, a substance has to go through the liquid state but in certain circumstances it can skip this step and turn straight from a solid into a gas. This is called sublimation. When the reverse happens, and a gas turns directly into a solid, it is known as deposition.

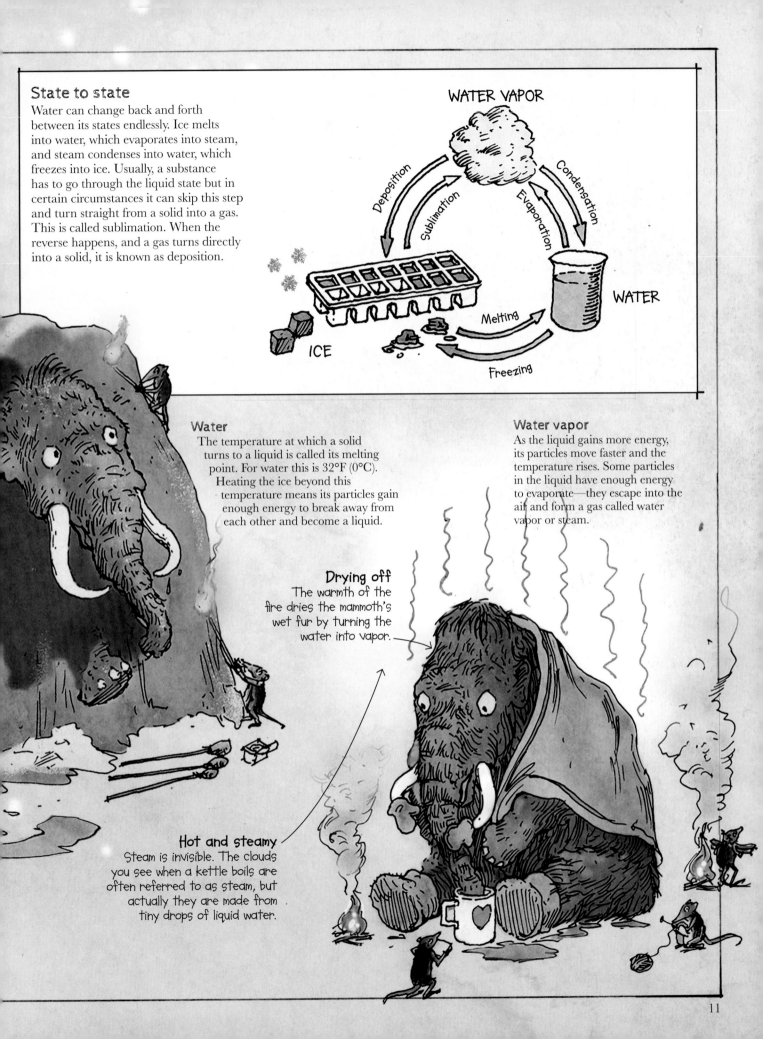

WATER VAPOR

Deposition

Sublimation

Condensation

Evaporation

WATER

Melting

ICE

Freezing

Water

The temperature at which a solid turns to a liquid is called its melting point. For water this is 32°F (0°C). Heating the ice beyond this temperature means its particles gain enough energy to break away from each other and become a liquid.

Water vapor

As the liquid gains more energy, its particles move faster and the temperature rises. Some particles in the liquid have enough energy to evaporate—they escape into the air and form a gas called water vapor or steam.

Drying off

The warmth of the fire dries the mammoth's wet fur by turning the water into vapor.

Hot and steamy

Steam is invisible. The clouds you see when a kettle boils are often referred to as steam, but actually they are made from tiny drops of liquid water.

11

Density

Matter makes up every object on the planet, but some things have more than others. Density is a measure of how much mass (amount of matter) an object has for its volume (how much space it takes up). Most solid objects are more dense because their particles are packed closely together. Liquids and gases tend to be less dense because their particles are more spread out.

Weighing it up

Three very different mammoths are standing on the scales. Although they may look similar in shape and size, the scales show that each mammoth has a different mass. This is because, despite each having the same volume, the three mammoths have wildly different densities.

Woolly mammoth
Lots of air is trapped between the individual strands of wool in this soft structure, making it much less dense than its flesh-and-bone double.

Real mammoth
A mammoth is made of a mixture of materials, such as hair and bone, which all together make it less dense than granite but denser than wool.

Granite mammoth
The strong stone of this sculpture is made up of particles that are very close together. Dense objects are heavier for their size—this one has smashed the scales!

Measuring density
To figure out the density of an object you need to know its mass and its volume. A simple hop on the scales will tell the mammoth its mass, but its complicated, irregular shape can make calculating volume a little more tricky. In cases like these, volume can be measured by a method called displacement.

Lower into tank
When a mammoth is submerged in water, some of the water will be displaced (pushed aside) to make room for it.

Water is displaced

Water level rises
The displaced water will have the same volume as the mammoth, and is much easier to measure.

Materials

All the objects around us are made of materials. Some materials, such as wood, metals, and ceramics, are made from substances found in nature. Others are made by chemical reactions. These are known as synthetic materials. Objects are often made from many different materials, each with its own useful properties.

Glass dome
A transparent glass window blocks out wind and rain without obscuring the view. Glass is made by heating sand with other chemicals.

Fiberglass fishing rods
Fiberglass is a light but strong composite material made of glass and plastic.

Gone fishing

An elephant shrew fishing trip is a mammoth undertaking. The shrews have carefully selected the right materials to construct their handcrafted vacation home. Each material has properties that can make it very good at some things and totally useless at others. Wood is hard and sturdy, so it makes a good material for the caravan's barrel-shaped body, but these same properties mean it would make a very uncomfortable mattress.

Rubber hose
Bendy rubber is a natural material that makes good tubing— flexible, lightweight, and waterproof.

Steel supports
Steel is a mixture of iron and carbon. It is heavy but very strong, so it's used where stable support is needed.

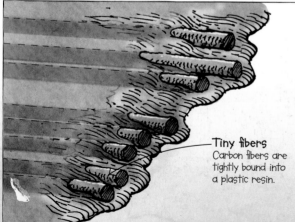

Tiny fibers
Carbon fibers are tightly bound into a plastic resin.

Composite materials

Combining two or more materials creates a composite material that can harness the most useful properties of each. An example is carbon fiber composite, which is made by weaving tiny strands of carbon together and surrounding them with plastic. Carbon fiber composite is strong but lightweight and resistant to heat. It is used to make the bodies of airplanes and racing cars.

Fabric shade
Light and soft, this fabric sheet can provide shade from the sun but not block out the light completely.

Aluminum frame
Aluminum is a metal that is light and easy to shape, so it is a good material for a lightweight frame. Sometimes it is mixed with other metals to make it stronger.

Plastic sheet
This plastic sheet makes a light, durable, and waterproof cover. Plastic is a synthetic material that can be molded and shaped into many different forms.

Wooden barrel
Wood is a natural material. It is readily available and widely used for building because it is strong and tough.

Rope
Rope is made from natural or synthetic fibers twisted together to form a strong cord that can be pulled on without snapping.

Vulcanized tires
Soft rubber is vulcanized (treated with chemicals) to make it harder.

15

Sandy mixture
The sludgy mix is a combination of salty sea water, sand, and bits of rock.

The biggest lumps are left in the sieve

Magnetism
A magnet would remove any iron particles in the sand.

Decanting the mixture leaves the sand lying at the bottom

Separated solids
Sieving, decanting, and filtration are ways of separating solid particles from a liquid. Decanting involves letting the solids settle at the bottom so the liquid can be poured off.

Filter paper
Tiny holes in the filter paper allow liquid through but not solid particles.

Salty solution
The filtered liquid is a mixture of water and salt.

Separating mixtures

A mixture is a combination of two or more substances jumbled together. Mixtures can be liquids, solids, gases, or a combination of these. The air we breathe is a mixture of different gases, while the sand on a beach is a mix of different solids. The key thing about mixtures is that they are not chemically combined—the particles of the substances are not joined together with chemical bonds. They can be separated again quite easily, if you know how.

Types of mixture

Salt water is a solution—a mixture where one substance (salt) is dissolved in another (water). The salt is so evenly mixed with the water that there are no visible particles: the salt seems to vanish into the water. Mixtures with visible particles, such as sandy water, are called suspensions. A mixture that looks evenly combined to the naked eye but actually contains tiny particles is called a colloid.

Solution
A beam of light will pass straight through a salt-water solution because there are no particles to reflect the light.

Colloid
Milk contains tiny fat droplets that catch the light, so if you shine a light through milk the path of light is clearly visible.

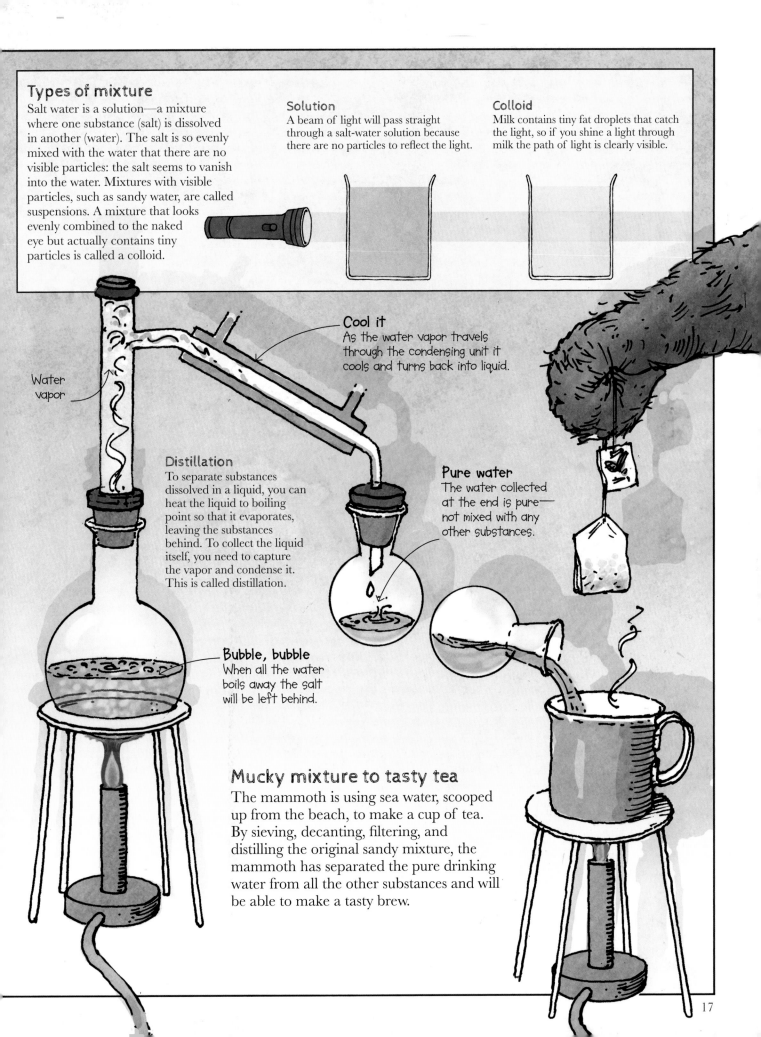

Water vapor

Cool it
As the water vapor travels through the condensing unit it cools and turns back into liquid.

Distillation
To separate substances dissolved in a liquid, you can heat the liquid to boiling point so that it evaporates, leaving the substances behind. To collect the liquid itself, you need to capture the vapor and condense it. This is called distillation.

Pure water
The water collected at the end is pure—not mixed with any other substances.

Bubble, bubble
When all the water boils away the salt will be left behind.

Mucky mixture to tasty tea
The mammoth is using sea water, scooped up from the beach, to make a cup of tea. By sieving, decanting, filtering, and distilling the original sandy mixture, the mammoth has separated the pure drinking water from all the other substances and will be able to make a tasty brew.

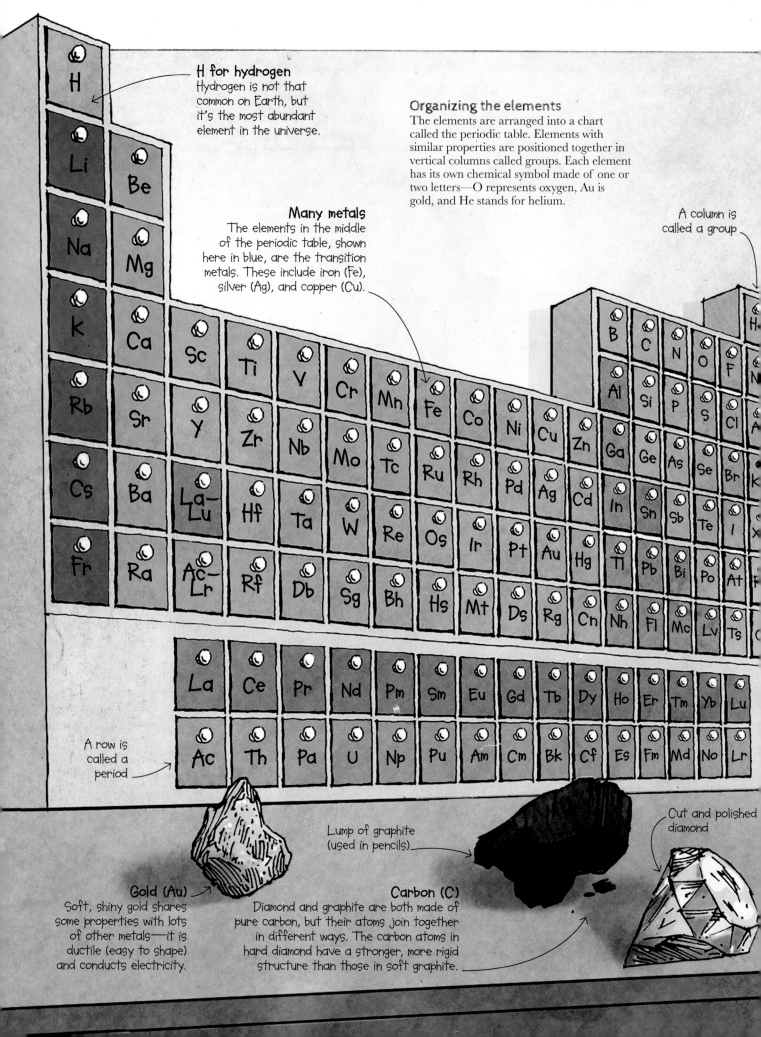

H for hydrogen
Hydrogen is not that common on Earth, but it's the most abundant element in the universe.

Organizing the elements
The elements are arranged into a chart called the periodic table. Elements with similar properties are positioned together in vertical columns called groups. Each element has its own chemical symbol made of one or two letters—O represents oxygen, Au is gold, and He stands for helium.

A column is called a group

Many metals
The elements in the middle of the periodic table, shown here in blue, are the transition metals. These include iron (Fe), silver (Ag), and copper (Cu).

A row is called a period

Gold (Au)
Soft, shiny gold shares some properties with lots of other metals—it is ductile (easy to shape) and conducts electricity.

Lump of graphite (used in pencils)

Carbon (C)
Diamond and graphite are both made of pure carbon, but their atoms join together in different ways. The carbon atoms in hard diamond have a stronger, more rigid structure than those in soft graphite.

Cut and polished diamond

Elements

Everything in the universe is made of matter. If you could break down matter into its simplest substances, you would be left with the elements. These are the building blocks of everything in the world, from mountains to mammoths. Most elements, such as oxygen and carbon, are found naturally on Earth, while others have been created by scientists in laboratories.

Examining the elements

Each element is made from just one type of atom (see pages 20–21). This gives every element its own properties. Most of the elements are solids at room temperature, and many of these are metals, such as iron and gold. Solid nonmetals include carbon and sulfur. Some elements are gases at room temperature—among these are oxygen, hydrogen, and helium.

What makes a mammoth?
Like all animals, mammoths are made up mostly of oxygen, carbon, and hydrogen. These three elements are the main ingredients in all living things.

Chlorine (Cl)
This pale green gas is very reactive (quick to join with other elements) and extremely poisonous.

Mercury (Hg)
This unusual metal is liquid at room temperature. It is beautiful to look at but gives off highly toxic fumes.

Atoms

Atoms are the minuscule building blocks that make up all matter. Everything you know is made from atoms—stars, books, mammoths, even your own body. Atoms are so tiny that seven billion of them could fit inside this punctuation. To build an atom you would need three even smaller types of particle: protons, neutrons, and electrons.

Under construction

This mammoth-built model shows the structure of an atom. The nucleus in the center is made up of protons and neutrons, while the excitable electrons whiz around outside in areas called shells. The attraction between the positively charged protons and negatively charged electrons is what holds the atom together.

Protons are positively charged

Electrons
These negatively charged particles are seriously tiny—nearly 2,000 times smaller than a proton or neutron.

Protons
Atoms have equal numbers of protons and electrons, so overall the atom has no charge.

Neutrons
These particles have no charge—they are neutral. They help bind the protons together inside the nucleus.

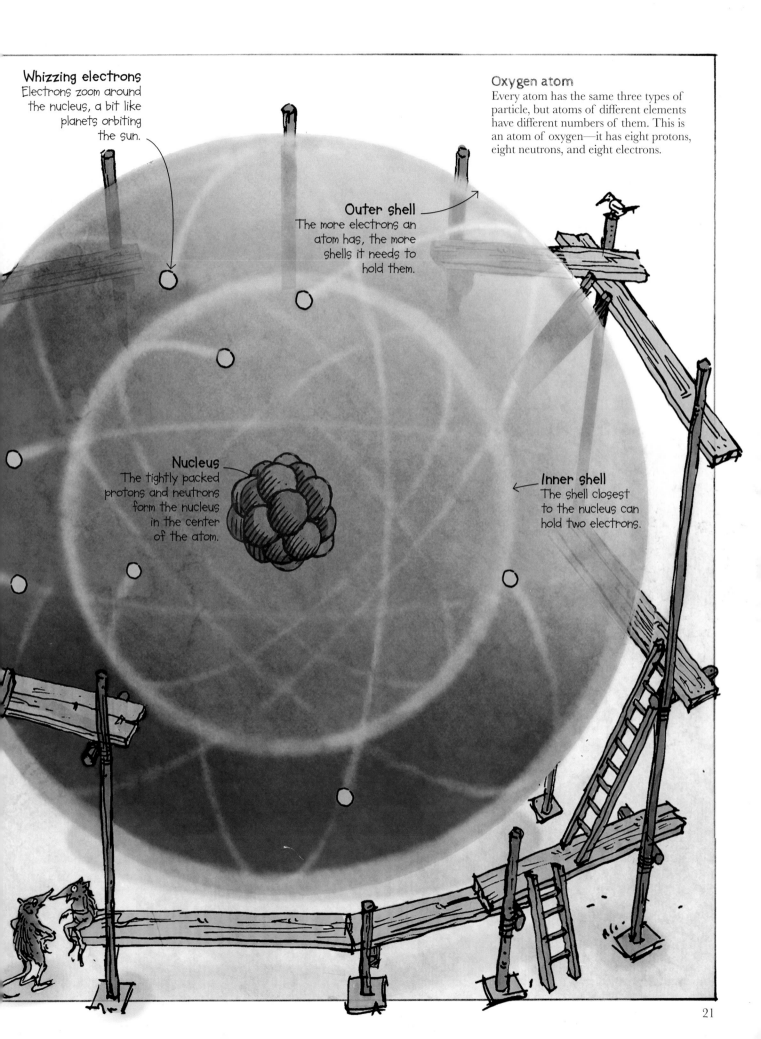

Whizzing electrons
Electrons zoom around the nucleus, a bit like planets orbiting the sun.

Oxygen atom
Every atom has the same three types of particle, but atoms of different elements have different numbers of them. This is an atom of oxygen—it has eight protons, eight neutrons, and eight electrons.

Outer shell
The more electrons an atom has, the more shells it needs to hold them.

Nucleus
The tightly packed protons and neutrons form the nucleus in the center of the atom.

Inner shell
The shell closest to the nucleus can hold two electrons.

21

Molecules

Two or more atoms joined together make a molecule. Molecules can be enormous, containing thousands of atoms, or they can be simple, made of just two or three. Some have only one type of atom: these are called elemental molecules. Others combine atoms of different elements to form compounds. The thing all molecules have in common is that they are held together by chemical bonds.

Construction complete

At this chemical construction site, two colorless gases have come together to form one of the mo important compounds on planet Earth: water. Vital for life as we know it, and great for quenching a thirst, all it takes to make a water molecule is an oxygen atom and two hydrogen atoms looking to form a bond.

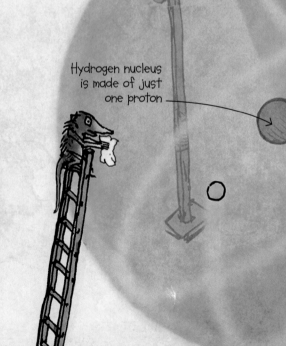

Hydrogen atom
Each hydrogen atom starts off with just one electron, but has space for two. Bonding with an oxygen atom completes each hydrogen atom's outer shell.

Hydrogen nucleus is made of just one proton

How chemical bonds work

The atoms in a molecule are bonded together because they share electrons. Atoms of each element (see pages 18–19) have a certain number of electrons. The electrons form shells around the nucleus. Each shell can hold a specific number of electrons. If the outer shell is not full, the atom can fill it up by sharing electrons with another atom. This creates a chemical bond between the two atoms.

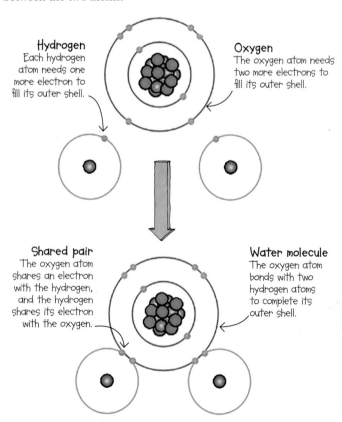

Hydrogen
Each hydrogen atom needs one more electron to fill its outer shell.

Oxygen
The oxygen atom needs two more electrons to fill its outer shell.

Shared pair
The oxygen atom shares an electron with the hydrogen, and the hydrogen shares its electron with the oxygen.

Water molecule
The oxygen atom bonds with two hydrogen atoms to complete its outer shell.

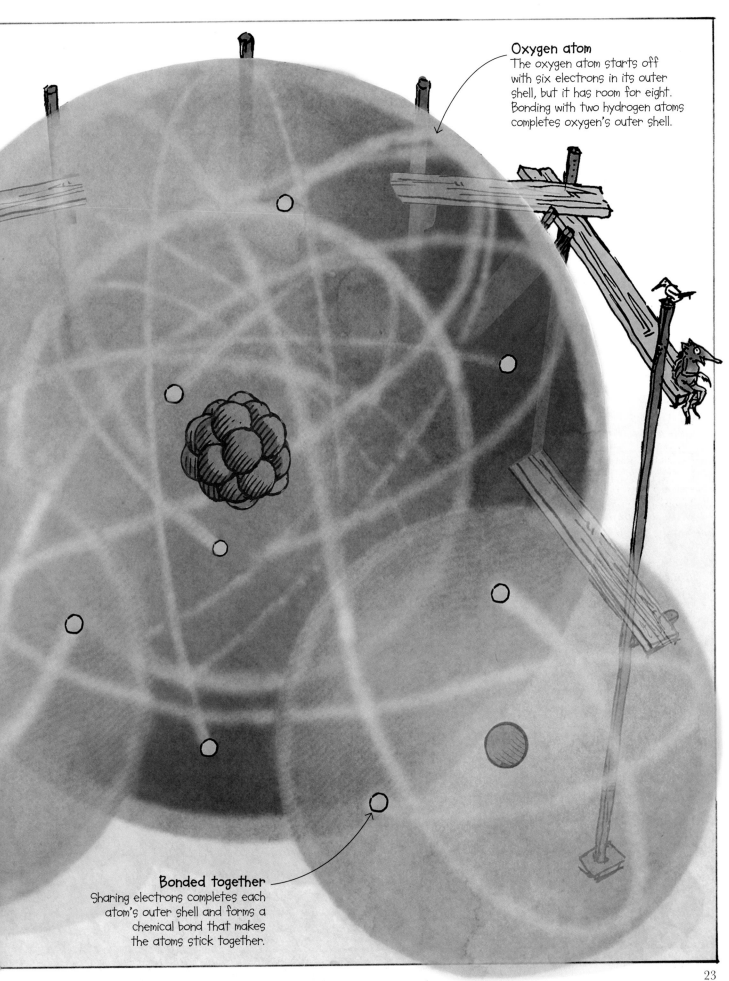

Oxygen atom
The oxygen atom starts off with six electrons in its outer shell, but it has room for eight. Bonding with two hydrogen atoms completes oxygen's outer shell.

Bonded together
Sharing electrons completes each atom's outer shell and forms a chemical bond that makes the atoms stick together.

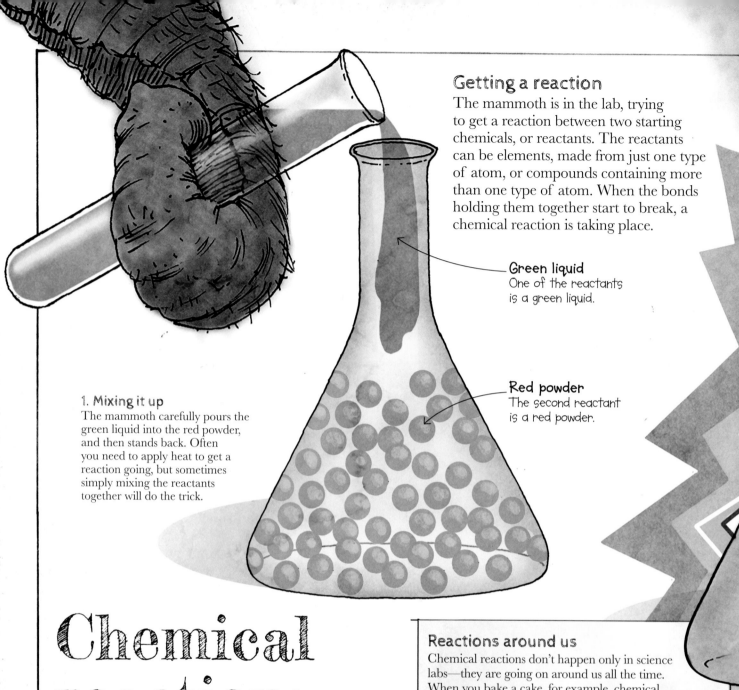

Getting a reaction

The mammoth is in the lab, trying to get a reaction between two starting chemicals, or reactants. The reactants can be elements, made from just one type of atom, or compounds containing more than one type of atom. When the bonds holding them together start to break, a chemical reaction is taking place.

Green liquid
One of the reactants is a green liquid.

Red powder
The second reactant is a red powder.

1. Mixing it up
The mammoth carefully pours the green liquid into the red powder, and then stands back. Often you need to apply heat to get a reaction going, but sometimes simply mixing the reactants together will do the trick.

Chemical reactions

When a solid melts into a liquid, the substance might look very different before and after. But melting is a physical change—the substance itself has not changed, only its physical state. Sometimes when you bring two substances together, a different kind of change can take place. The atoms and molecules of the substances reshuffle and recombine to form a completely different end product. This is called a chemical reaction.

Reactions around us
Chemical reactions don't happen only in science labs—they are going on around us all the time. When you bake a cake, for example, chemical reactions turn the raw ingredients from a sloppy cake mixture to a brand new (and delicious) substance: cake. Then when you eat the cake, chemical reactions in your stomach help digest it.

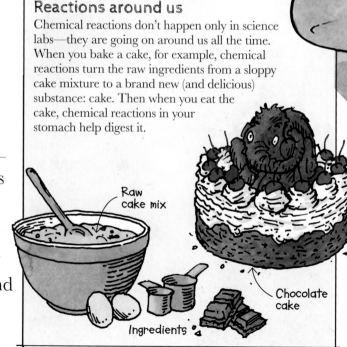

Raw cake mix

Chocolate cake

Ingredients

Wisps of gas
The reaction has also produced a gas. No atoms are created or destroyed in a chemical reaction. All the atoms that were present in the reactants will be in the end products.

Heat and light
These are signs that a chemical reaction is taking place.

2. Whiz, pop, bang!
As soon as the two substances mix, they start to react with each other. The chemical bonds between their atoms and molecules break and reform.

New substance
One of the products is a yellow powder.

3. End product
The substance produced by a chemical reaction is called the product. The product can be very different from the original reactants that went into it.

Rapid reactions

Some chemical reactions happen very slowly, while others take place in the blink of an eye. Explosions are very quick reactions that release a lot of heat, light, and sound. They release gases so quickly that they can blow things apart. Fireworks use controlled explosions and colorful chemical reactions to create a dazzling light show in the night sky.

Dazzling display
The different colors are produced by the "stars" packed into the rocket's chamber. These are metals that burn with different colored light.

Rapid rocket
The gunpowder propels the rocket into the air in an instant.

1. Outer fuse
The outer fuse burns slowly, to give the person who lit it time to stand back.

2. Fast side fuse
The long side fuse burns quickly, igniting the gunpowder and launching the rocket into the air.

"Stars" of different colors

Gunpowder

Launching tube

3. Slow central fuse
The central fuse burns slowly, only igniting the gunpowder and stars once the rocket is high in the air.

Rocket reactions

When a firework goes off, several rapid reactions happen. The burning fuse ignites a store of gunpowder, which explodes to send the rocket flying into the sky. Once in the air, another explosion ignites the "stars"—metal pieces that burn with bright colors and sparks.

Slow reactions

Rusting is an example of a slow reaction. If you leave a metal bike outside, over time it will show signs of rust. This is because iron in the bike's metal frame reacts with water and oxygen in the air to form flaky, orange iron oxide, or rust. This corrodes the metal—eventually it will crumble completely.

Combustion

The flame from a cozy campfire provides light and heat—more than enough to toast a marshmallow or two. When a fire burns, a chemical reaction called combustion is taking place. Combustion releases energy, and produces water, carbon dioxide, and sometimes other chemicals, too. It is one of the most useful reactions for humans, but it can easily get out of control. Happily, these mammoth fire wardens are standing by.

Fire blanket
Smothering the flame with a blanket stops oxygen reaching the fire.

Oxygen
Fires need oxygen to keep burning. The air around us is 20 percent oxygen—more than enough to sustain a roaring fire. There is oxygen in our breath, too, so when you gently blow air into embers, they glow bright orange as the fire gets stronger.

The fire triangle

Fire always needs three things to get going and stay burning: oxygen, fuel, and heat. This is known as the fire triangle. We can use this knowledge to build a roaring fire, but also to put it out again: taking away any of the three sides of the triangle extinguishes the fire.

Essential oxygen

When there is plenty of oxygen available, the substances produced by combustion are water and carbon dioxide, a harmless gas. But when there is not enough oxygen, incomplete combustion can occur. Some of the fuel turns to soot and a dangerous gas called carbon monoxide. The color of the flame can indicate whether complete or incomplete combustion is taking place.

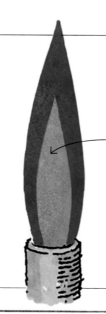

Bunsen burner
The blue flame of a Bunsen burner is an example of complete combustion.

Sooty candle
A yellow flame is a sign of incomplete combustion.

OXYGEN

HEAT

FUEL

Spraying with water
Dousing with water takes away the heat so the fire goes out.

Heat
Luckily, fuel and oxygen on their own aren't enough to start a fire, or trees would be bursting into flames every day. You need heat to start the reaction, but then once it gets going the fire provides its own heat.

Fuel
The material that burns is called the fuel. Lots of things can be used as fuel, including wood, paper, and wax. Some fuels burn much more easily than others: a piece of wood will burn slowly but gasoline will go up in flames in a flash.

Removing the fuel
Without fuel to keep the reaction going, the fire sputters and dies.

Low numbers
Numbers lower than 7 are acidic.

Higher numbers
Higher than 7 and a substance is alkaline.

0 1 2 3 4 5 6 7 8 9 10 11 12 13 14

acid

alkali

The pH scale
If you don't have a mammoth handy, you can test pH in a more traditional way. Universal indicator is a mixture of chemicals that changes color to indicate pH level, with the colors usually matching the chart above.

Lemon
At pH 3, lemons are very acidic, which is why they taste so sour.

The pH scale

An important property of any substance is its acidity. Weak acids are found in many foods and taste sour, while strong acids can eat through metal or damage skin. The opposite of an acid is a base. Bases that can dissolve in water are called alkalies. They usually taste bitter and may be used as cleaning products because they attack fats and oils. Strong alkalies can be as dangerous as strong acids.

Acid or alkali?

The items on the conveyor belt are being tested to see if they are acids or alkalies. Scientists use the pH scale to measure this. The pH scale goes from 0 to 14, with low numbers being acidic, high numbers being alkaline, and 7 being neutral. If you mix an acid with an alkali, they cancel each other out and become neutral.

Esophagus
Food travels from the mouth to the stomach through a tube called the esophagus.

Stomach

Stomach lining
The acid is created by cells in the lining of the stomach.

Food
Food is broken down by the acidic juices, forming a pulpy mass.

Stomach acid

There are some powerful acids inside the human body. The stomach produces hydrochloric acid, which helps digest food and kills off any harmful bugs. The pH of stomach acid is usually between 1.5 and 3.5, so the stomach walls are protected from the acid by a layer of sticky mucus (which also stops stomach acid digesting the stomach itself).

Laundry powder
Laundry powder is a base—a solid substance that forms an alkali when it dissolves in water.

Water
Water is usually neutral, at pH 7.

Milk
Milk is a tiny bit acidic, at pH 6.5.

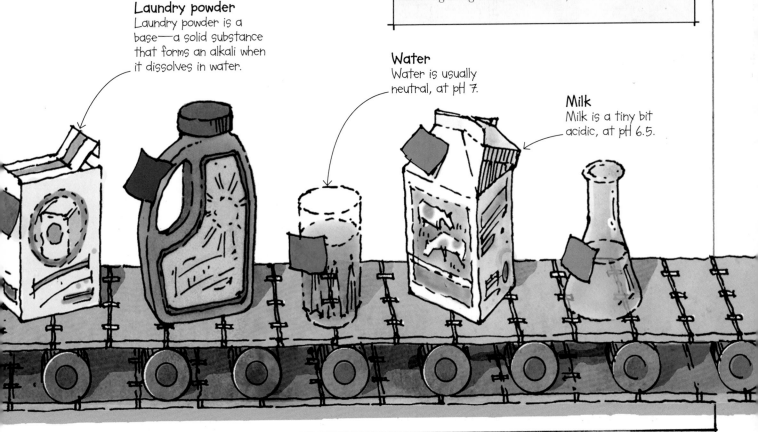

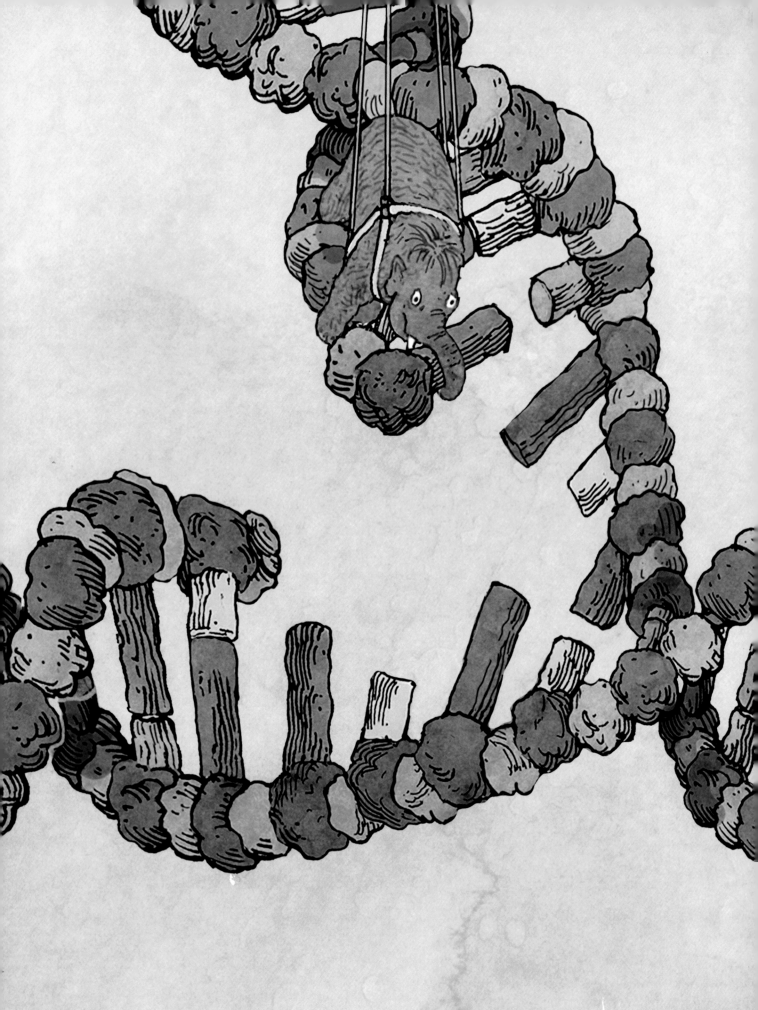

Life

Life on Earth comes in all shapes and sizes, from plants and toadstools and seaweed to you reading this book right now. Although living things may look different, they share some specific characteristics that set them apart from nonliving things.

Kingdoms of life

Scientists have discovered almost two million different species of living things so far, ranging from tiny bacteria to whales and giant trees. All these forms of life are placed into seven major divisions, called kingdoms.

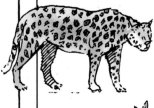

Animals

This kingdom includes mammals, birds, reptiles, frogs and toads, fish, insects, spiders, and worms. Animals eat other organisms and have muscles and nerves that help them move and respond.

Plants

There are more than 390,000 different types of plant, from tiny weeds to gigantic forest trees. Most have leaves and many have flowers or cones. They use sunlight to make their own food.

Fungi

Neither plants nor animals, fungi include mushrooms and toadstools. Most of them grow in damp places, such as woodland floors or on rotten wood.

Algae

Often found in water, algae include seaweeds. Many look similar to plants and, in the same way as plants, make their own food by using sunlight.

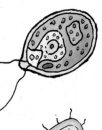

Protozoans

These tiny, single-celled organisms live in water, damp soil, or even inside animals and plants. Some use hairlike threads to "swim" around.

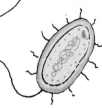

Bacteria

Bacteria have many different shapes, but all are made of a single cell that lacks a nucleus. They can live almost anywhere. You probably have about 100 trillion of them in or on your body.

Archaea

Archaea are similar to bacteria— their single cells do not have a nucleus. Many archaea can survive in much hotter, colder, saltier, or more airless places than other forms of life.

Sensing surroundings

Being able to respond to your surroundings means you are definitely alive. Spotting the saber-toothed cat in the grass will help this mammoth stay that way!

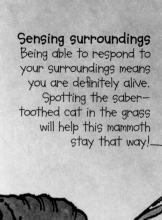

Checklist for life

These munching mammoths show the seven characteristics shared by all living things. They grow and change, move around, get rid of waste, and can reproduce themselves. They can sense and respond to their surroundings. They take in nutrients from food and use them to release energy inside their cells in a process called respiration.

Respiration
Animals breathe in oxygen to power respiration in their cells.

Grabbing grub
All life forms need nutrients for cell growth and energy.

On the move
A galumphing mammoth is hard to miss but some life forms move more subtly. Plants can turn toward light.

Removing waste
Living things rid their bodies of waste products.

Growing and changing
Things made of living cells develop and grow, though they don't all reach jumbo size.

Mini me
Reproducing ensures that life goes on.

Bacteria

Bacteria are the smallest living things on Earth. They can multiply very quickly, and there are so many trillions of them in the world it would be impossible to count them. They are found just about everywhere: in soil, water, and the air around you, inside your body and on its surface, too. Each bacterium is made of just one cell, with a very simple structure.

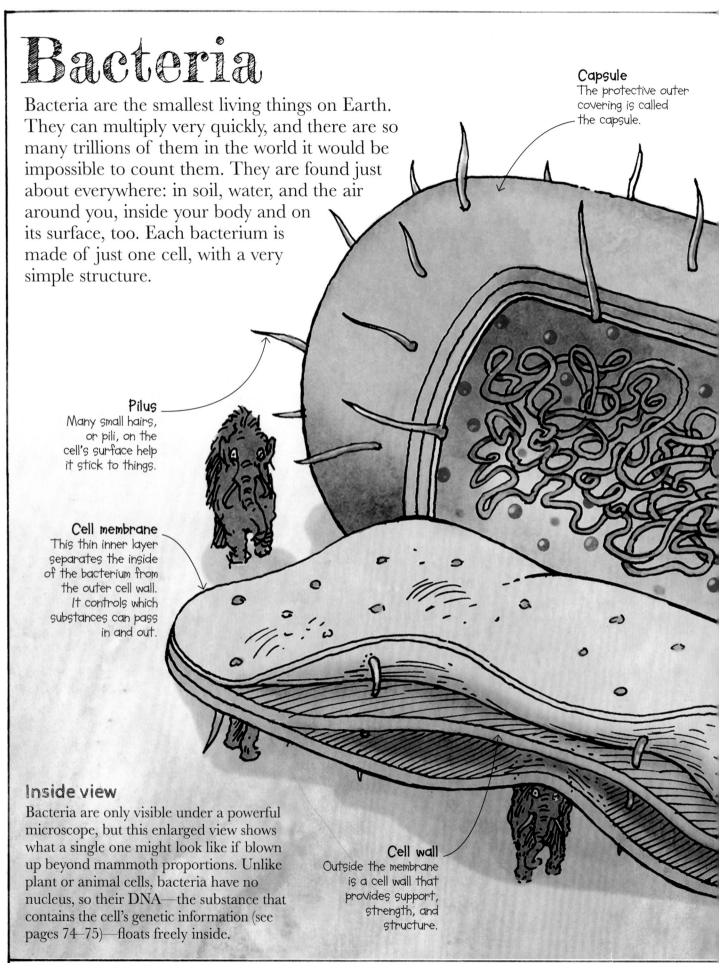

Capsule
The protective outer covering is called the capsule.

Pilus
Many small hairs, or pili, on the cell's surface help it stick to things.

Cell membrane
This thin inner layer separates the inside of the bacterium from the outer cell wall. It controls which substances can pass in and out.

Cell wall
Outside the membrane is a cell wall that provides support, strength, and structure.

Inside view

Bacteria are only visible under a powerful microscope, but this enlarged view shows what a single one might look like if blown up beyond mammoth proportions. Unlike plant or animal cells, bacteria have no nucleus, so their DNA—the substance that contains the cell's genetic information (see pages 74–75)—floats freely inside.

36

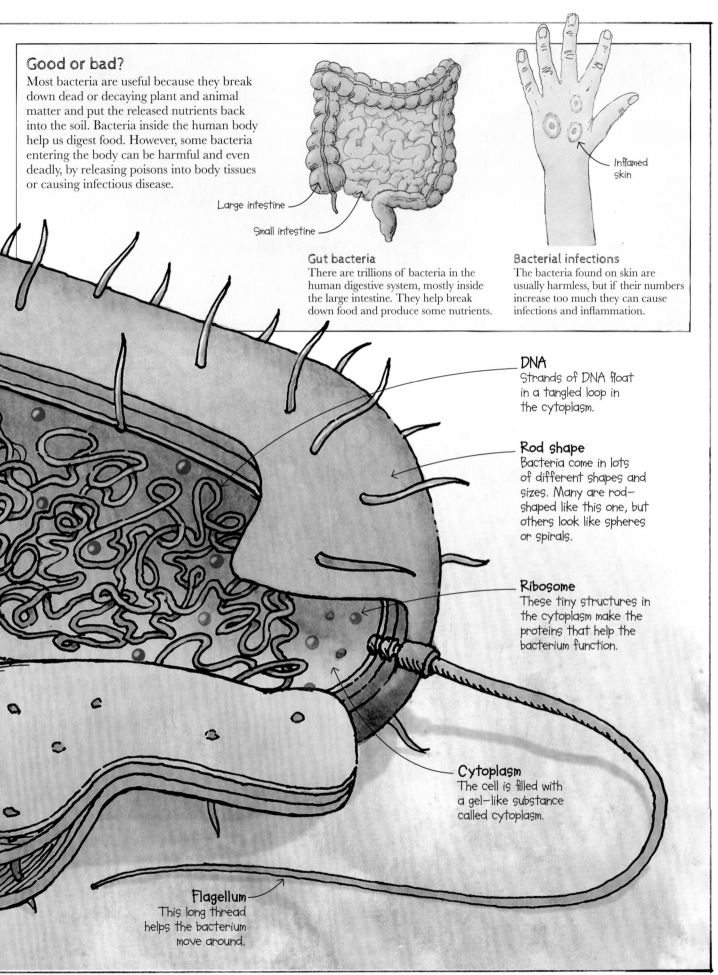

Good or bad?

Most bacteria are useful because they break down dead or decaying plant and animal matter and put the released nutrients back into the soil. Bacteria inside the human body help us digest food. However, some bacteria entering the body can be harmful and even deadly, by releasing poisons into body tissues or causing infectious disease.

Large intestine

Small intestine

Inflamed skin

Gut bacteria
There are trillions of bacteria in the human digestive system, mostly inside the large intestine. They help break down food and produce some nutrients.

Bacterial infections
The bacteria found on skin are usually harmless, but if their numbers increase too much they can cause infections and inflammation.

DNA
Strands of DNA float in a tangled loop in the cytoplasm.

Rod shape
Bacteria come in lots of different shapes and sizes. Many are rod-shaped like this one, but others look like spheres or spirals.

Ribosome
These tiny structures in the cytoplasm make the proteins that help the bacterium function.

Cytoplasm
The cell is filled with a gel-like substance called cytoplasm.

Flagellum
This long thread helps the bacterium move around.

Cells

Every living thing on Earth is made up of tiny units called cells, which are so small that they can only be seen with a microscope. Some living things, such as bacteria, only have one cell. Others, such as plants and big, bulky woolly mammoths, have trillions and trillions of cells.

Animal cell

Each cell in a mammoth's trunk is a tiny powerhouse. The nucleus is the control center of the cell and contains all of the instructions for how the cell should work. Mitochondria power the cell by releasing energy. Cells are surrounded by a thin, oily cell membrane, and are filled with a jelly-like fluid called the cytoplasm.

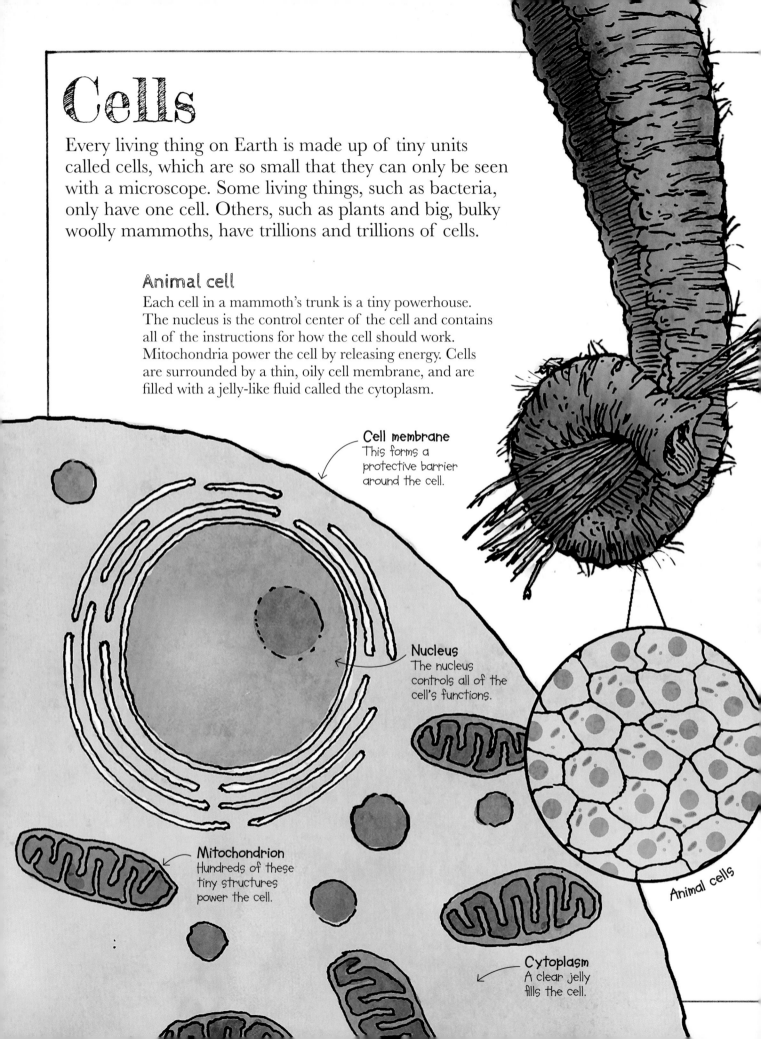

Cell membrane
This forms a protective barrier around the cell.

Nucleus
The nucleus controls all of the cell's functions.

Mitochondrion
Hundreds of these tiny structures power the cell.

Cytoplasm
A clear jelly fills the cell.

Animal cells

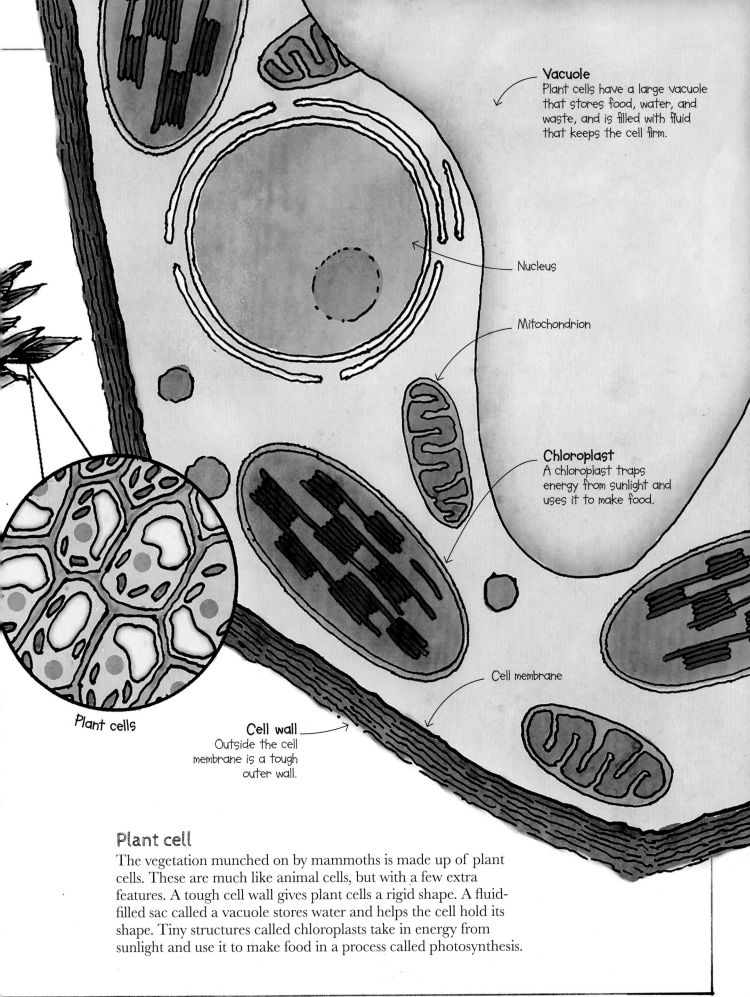

Vacuole
Plant cells have a large vacuole that stores food, water, and waste, and is filled with fluid that keeps the cell firm.

Nucleus

Mitochondrion

Chloroplast
A chloroplast traps energy from sunlight and uses it to make food.

Cell membrane

Plant cells

Cell wall
Outside the cell membrane is a tough outer wall.

Plant cell

The vegetation munched on by mammoths is made up of plant cells. These are much like animal cells, but with a few extra features. A tough cell wall gives plant cells a rigid shape. A fluid-filled sac called a vacuole stores water and helps the cell hold its shape. Tiny structures called chloroplasts take in energy from sunlight and use it to make food in a process called photosynthesis.

Types of cell

Although they share the same basic parts, the trillions of cells that make up a living organism are not all the same. Cells come in many different shapes and sizes, with special features to allow them to do specific jobs. The human body contains more than 200 different types of cell, each with its own special function.

Cells on parade

Quick march! This unusual procession features just a few of the cells found in the human body. There is a wide variety of shapes and sizes on display, but the cells here aren't shown to scale. In reality, the egg cell is about 10 times bigger than the other cells on parade and the threadlike axons of nerve cells can stretch up to 3 ft (1 m) long.

Epithelial cell
These are arranged in sheets to form a protective barrier. The skin is made of epithelial cells.

Some epithelial cells have a brushlike surface to absorb fluids and nutrients

Egg cell
The largest human body cell is the female sex cell. When fertilized by a sperm cell, it grows into a baby.

Sperm cell
The male sex cell is the smallest human body cell. It has a long tail to help it swim to the egg.

Red blood cell
Disk-shaped red blood cells transport oxygen around the body.

White blood cell
This circular cell moves around the bloodstream killing germs.

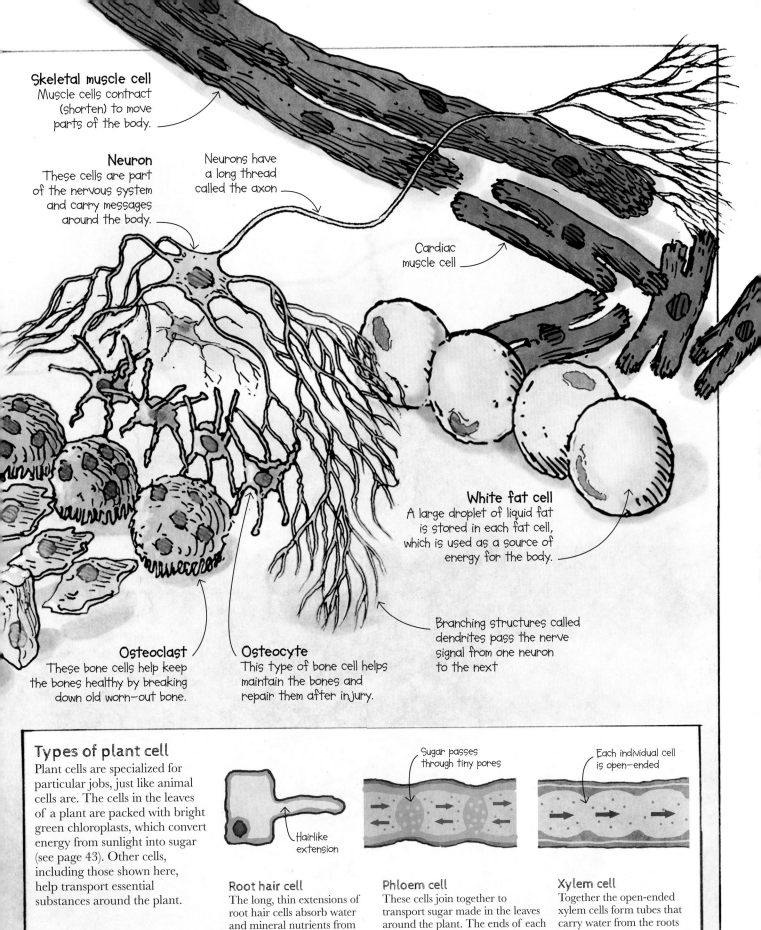

Skeletal muscle cell
Muscle cells contract (shorten) to move parts of the body.

Neuron
These cells are part of the nervous system and carry messages around the body.

Neurons have a long thread called the axon

Cardiac muscle cell

White fat cell
A large droplet of liquid fat is stored in each fat cell, which is used as a source of energy for the body.

Branching structures called dendrites pass the nerve signal from one neuron to the next

Osteoclast
These bone cells help keep the bones healthy by breaking down old worn-out bone.

Osteocyte
This type of bone cell helps maintain the bones and repair them after injury.

Types of plant cell

Plant cells are specialized for particular jobs, just like animal cells are. The cells in the leaves of a plant are packed with bright green chloroplasts, which convert energy from sunlight into sugar (see page 43). Other cells, including those shown here, help transport essential substances around the plant.

Hairlike extension

Sugar passes through tiny pores

Each individual cell is open-ended

Root hair cell
The long, thin extensions of root hair cells absorb water and mineral nutrients from the soil.

Phloem cell
These cells join together to transport sugar made in the leaves around the plant. The ends of each cell have tiny pores (openings).

Xylem cell
Together the open-ended xylem cells form tubes that carry water from the roots to the stem and leaves.

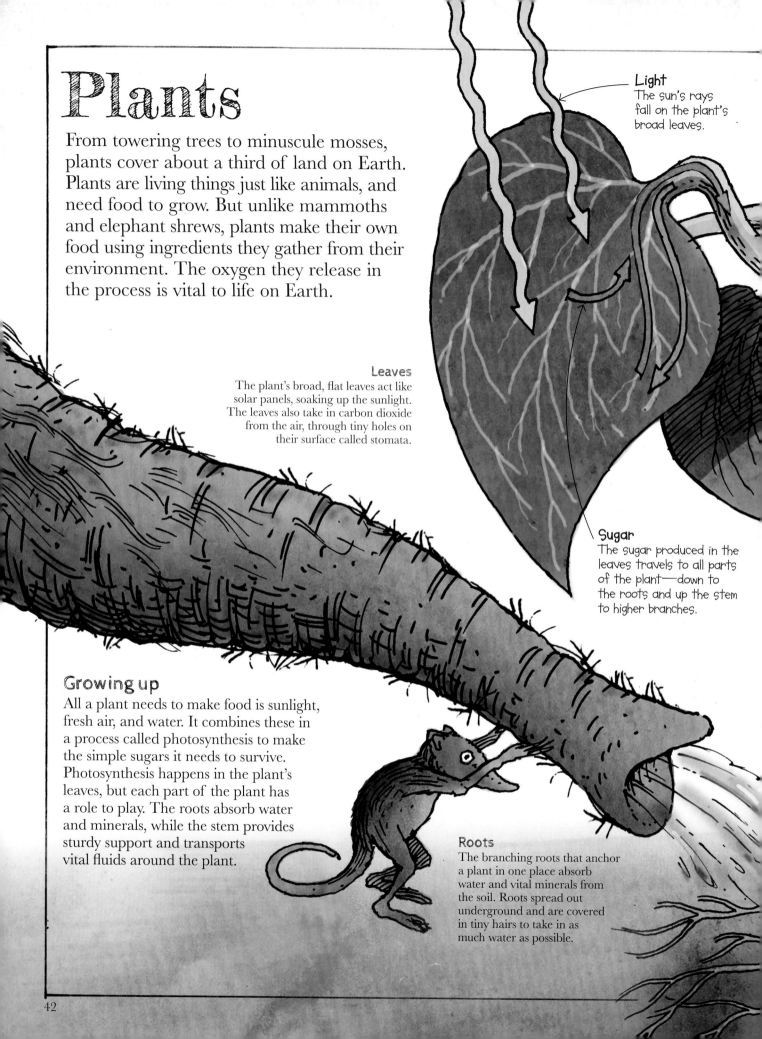

Plants

From towering trees to minuscule mosses, plants cover about a third of land on Earth. Plants are living things just like animals, and need food to grow. But unlike mammoths and elephant shrews, plants make their own food using ingredients they gather from their environment. The oxygen they release in the process is vital to life on Earth.

Light
The sun's rays fall on the plant's broad leaves.

Leaves
The plant's broad, flat leaves act like solar panels, soaking up the sunlight. The leaves also take in carbon dioxide from the air, through tiny holes on their surface called stomata.

Sugar
The sugar produced in the leaves travels to all parts of the plant—down to the roots and up the stem to higher branches.

Growing up
All a plant needs to make food is sunlight, fresh air, and water. It combines these in a process called photosynthesis to make the simple sugars it needs to survive. Photosynthesis happens in the plant's leaves, but each part of the plant has a role to play. The roots absorb water and minerals, while the stem provides sturdy support and transports vital fluids around the plant.

Roots
The branching roots that anchor a plant in one place absorb water and vital minerals from the soil. Roots spread out underground and are covered in tiny hairs to take in as much water as possible.

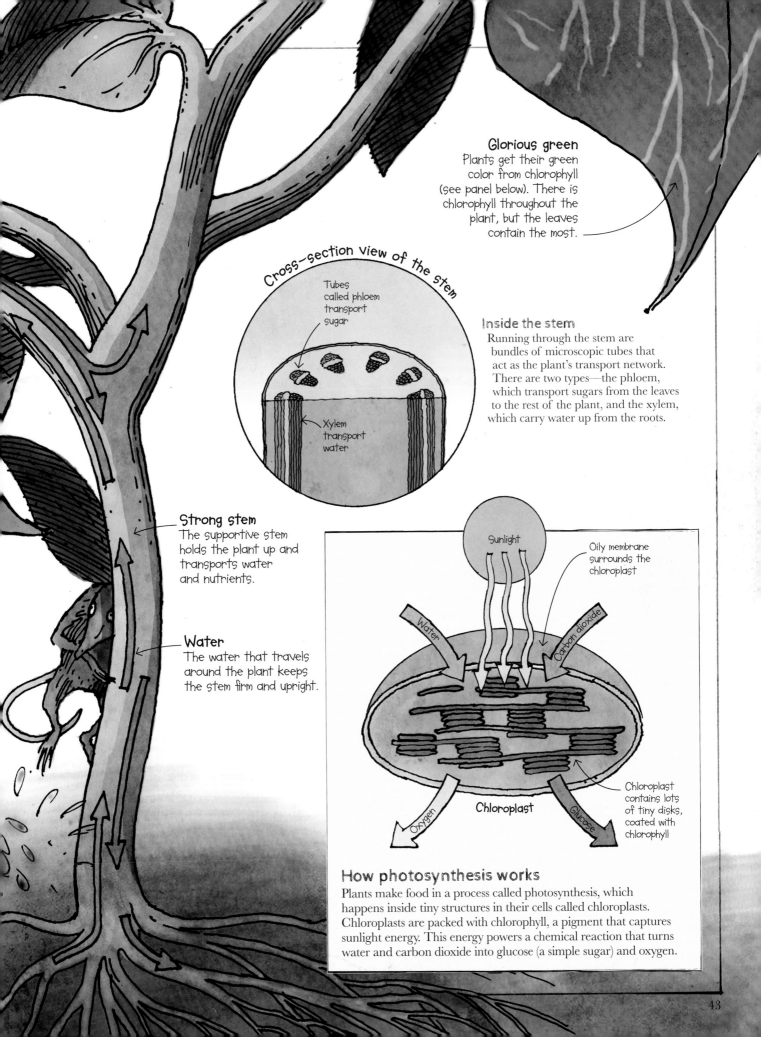

Glorious green
Plants get their green color from chlorophyll (see panel below). There is chlorophyll throughout the plant, but the leaves contain the most.

Cross-section view of the stem

Tubes called phloem transport sugar

Xylem transport water

Inside the stem
Running through the stem are bundles of microscopic tubes that act as the plant's transport network. There are two types—the phloem, which transport sugars from the leaves to the rest of the plant, and the xylem, which carry water up from the roots.

Strong stem
The supportive stem holds the plant up and transports water and nutrients.

Water
The water that travels around the plant keeps the stem firm and upright.

Sunlight

Oily membrane surrounds the chloroplast

Water

Carbon dioxide

Oxygen

Chloroplast

Glucose

Chloroplast contains lots of tiny disks, coated with chlorophyll

How photosynthesis works
Plants make food in a process called photosynthesis, which happens inside tiny structures in their cells called chloroplasts. Chloroplasts are packed with chlorophyll, a pigment that captures sunlight energy. This energy powers a chemical reaction that turns water and carbon dioxide into glucose (a simple sugar) and oxygen.

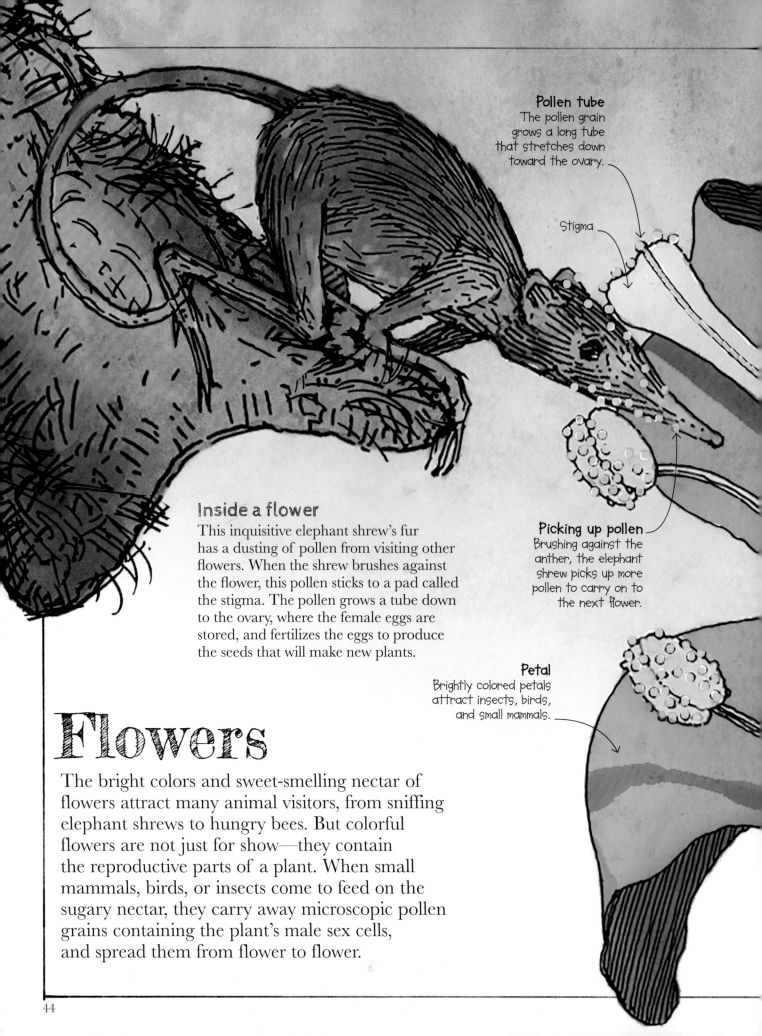

Pollen tube
The pollen grain grows a long tube that stretches down toward the ovary.

Stigma

Picking up pollen
Brushing against the anther, the elephant shrew picks up more pollen to carry on to the next flower.

Inside a flower
This inquisitive elephant shrew's fur has a dusting of pollen from visiting other flowers. When the shrew brushes against the flower, this pollen sticks to a pad called the stigma. The pollen grows a tube down to the ovary, where the female eggs are stored, and fertilizes the eggs to produce the seeds that will make new plants.

Petal
Brightly colored petals attract insects, birds, and small mammals.

Flowers

The bright colors and sweet-smelling nectar of flowers attract many animal visitors, from sniffing elephant shrews to hungry bees. But colorful flowers are not just for show—they contain the reproductive parts of a plant. When small mammals, birds, or insects come to feed on the sugary nectar, they carry away microscopic pollen grains containing the plant's male sex cells, and spread them from flower to flower.

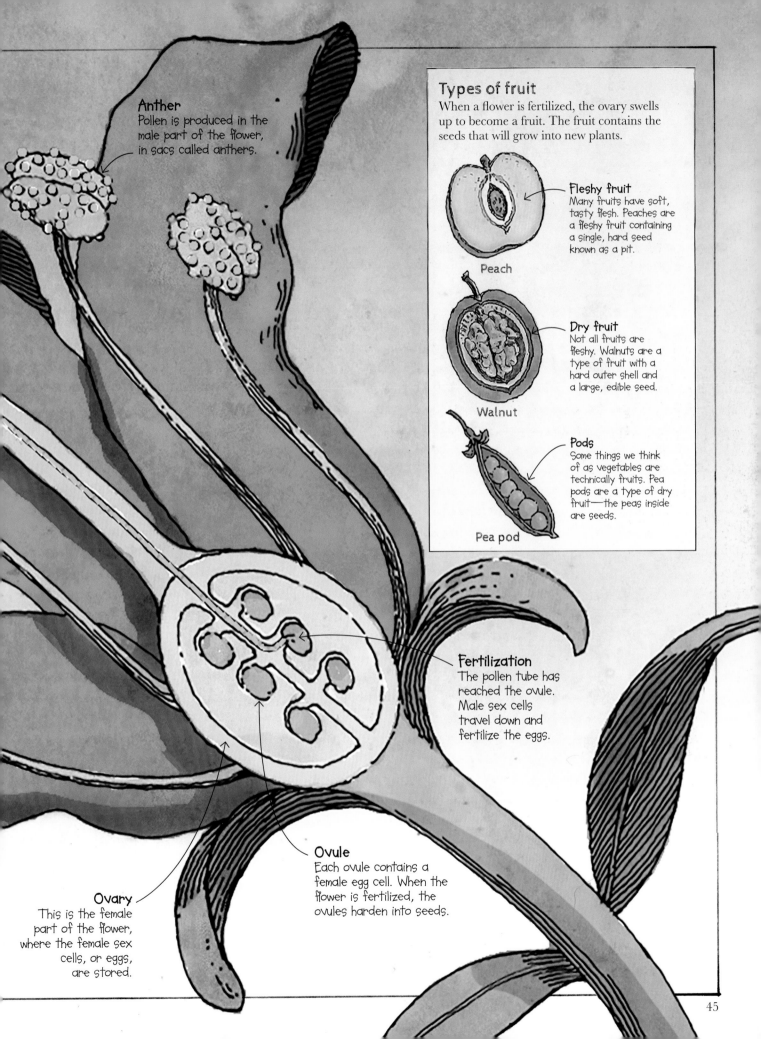

Anther
Pollen is produced in the male part of the flower, in sacs called anthers.

Types of fruit
When a flower is fertilized, the ovary swells up to become a fruit. The fruit contains the seeds that will grow into new plants.

Peach

Fleshy fruit
Many fruits have soft, tasty flesh. Peaches are a fleshy fruit containing a single, hard seed known as a pit.

Walnut

Dry fruit
Not all fruits are fleshy. Walnuts are a type of fruit with a hard outer shell and a large, edible seed.

Pea pod

Pods
Some things we think of as vegetables are technically fruits. Pea pods are a type of dry fruit—the peas inside are seeds.

Fertilization
The pollen tube has reached the ovule. Male sex cells travel down and fertilize the eggs.

Ovule
Each ovule contains a female egg cell. When the flower is fertilized, the ovules harden into seeds.

Ovary
This is the female part of the flower, where the female sex cells, or eggs, are stored.

Going traveling

Some seeds are light enough to be blown on the wind or tough enough to float on water. Others rely on animals for a ride. Many have pods that explode, flinging their contents away from the parent plant.

Coconut

Dandelion seed

Sailing away
Some large seeds have a waterproof coating and are carried on water. Coconuts can even float on ocean currents.

Airborne
Small, lightweight seeds are carried away on the slightest breeze.

Hitching a ride
Some seeds have prickly hairs or hooks that stick to animal fur.

Big bang
Many plants, such as peas, have seed pods that burst open to shoot out the seeds.

Prickly burr seeds

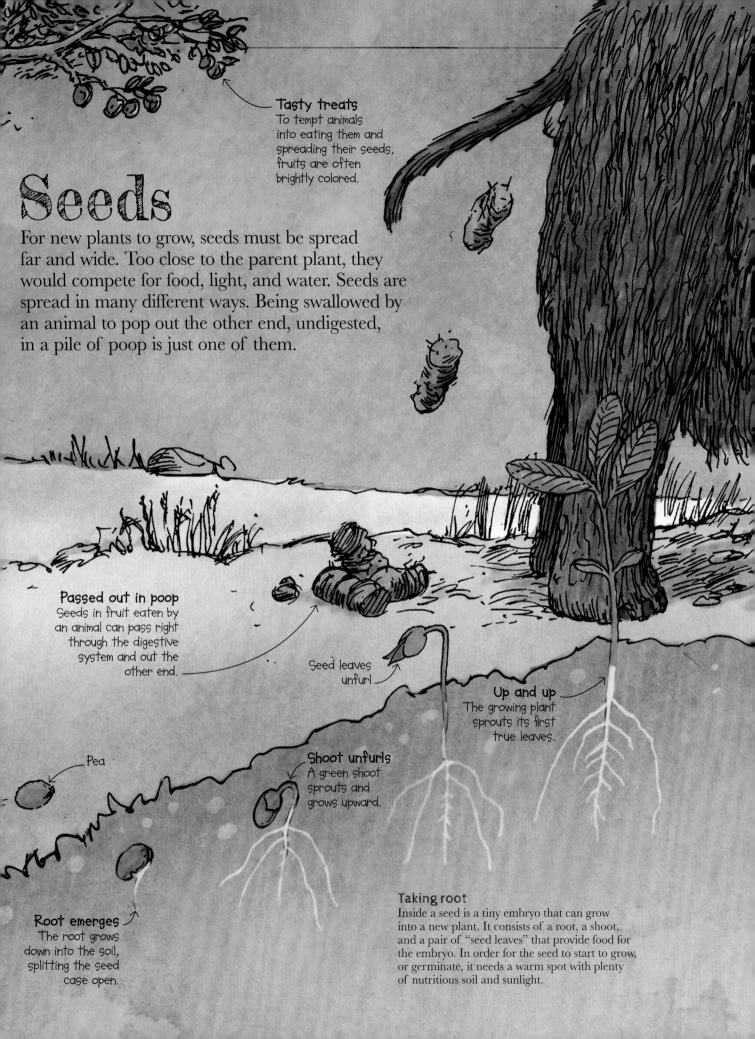

Seeds

For new plants to grow, seeds must be spread far and wide. Too close to the parent plant, they would compete for food, light, and water. Seeds are spread in many different ways. Being swallowed by an animal to pop out the other end, undigested, in a pile of poop is just one of them.

Tasty treats
To tempt animals into eating them and spreading their seeds, fruits are often brightly colored.

Passed out in poop
Seeds in fruit eaten by an animal can pass right through the digestive system and out the other end.

Seed leaves unfurl

Up and up
The growing plant sprouts its first true leaves.

Pea

Shoot unfurls
A green shoot sprouts and grows upward.

Root emerges
The root grows down into the soil, splitting the seed case open.

Taking root
Inside a seed is a tiny embryo that can grow into a new plant. It consists of a root, a shoot, and a pair of "seed leaves" that provide food for the embryo. In order for the seed to start to grow, or germinate, it needs a warm spot with plenty of nutritious soil and sunlight.

Food chains

Life on Earth is linked because plants and animals provide food for each other. In this prehistoric scene, grass is munched by a mammoth who is watching out for hungry predators ready to pounce. This is an example of a food chain. Grass is a plentiful source of food at the bottom of the chain, while the saber-toothed cat sits comfortably at the top facing no threats at all.

Munching mammoth
Animals that eat producers are called primary consumers. They form the second step in the food chain. Here, energy stored in the grass is passing into the body of the mammoth.

Sunlight
The sun is the original source of energy in almost all food chains.

Green grass
At the bottom of the food chain are the producers. Usually these are green plants that combine energy from sunlight with nutrients in the soil to create their own food through photosynthesis (see pages 42–43).

Flow of energy
All living things need energy from food to survive. In a food chain, energy passes from one organism to another. Plants harness energy from the sun, which passes to the animals that eat the grass. When those animals are themselves eaten, the energy flows up the chain.

Hungry hunter

If the mammoth gets munched, then energy will pass to the saber-toothed cat. Animals that eat other animals are called secondary consumers. Cats eat only meat, but some secondary consumers eat plants as well, making them primary and secondary consumers.

Dung beetle

This decomposer feeds on poop produced by other animals.

Food webs

Most creatures play a part in more than one food chain. Interlinking food chains form a complex network called a food web, which shows how energy flows between animals in a particular habitat. In this Arctic food web, the producers are tiny photosynthesizing algae known as phytoplankton.

Top predator
The killer whale is at the top of the food web, with no natural predators.

Killer whale

Harbor seal

Ringed seal

Arctic char

Krill

Harp seal

Arctic cod

Capelin

Polar bear

Arctic tern

Producers
Microscopic phytoplankton harness energy from the sun.

Phytoplankton

Decomposer

Creatures that feed on waste and dead organisms are called decomposers. They break down decaying animals and return nutrients to the soil for plants to use, which keeps energy flowing.

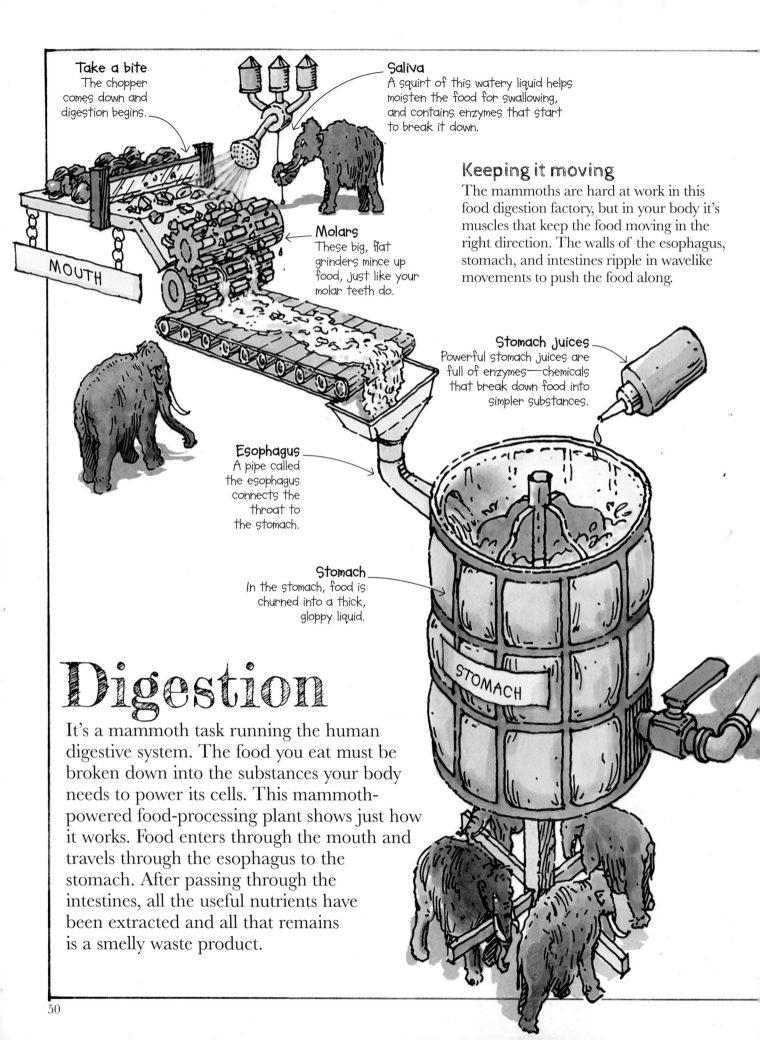

Take a bite
The chopper comes down and digestion begins.

Saliva
A squirt of this watery liquid helps moisten the food for swallowing, and contains enzymes that start to break it down.

Molars
These big, flat grinders mince up food, just like your molar teeth do.

MOUTH

Keeping it moving
The mammoths are hard at work in this food digestion factory, but in your body it's muscles that keep the food moving in the right direction. The walls of the esophagus, stomach, and intestines ripple in wavelike movements to push the food along.

Stomach juices
Powerful stomach juices are full of enzymes—chemicals that break down food into simpler substances.

Esophagus
A pipe called the esophagus connects the throat to the stomach.

Stomach
In the stomach, food is churned into a thick, gloppy liquid.

STOMACH

Digestion

It's a mammoth task running the human digestive system. The food you eat must be broken down into the substances your body needs to power its cells. This mammoth-powered food-processing plant shows just how it works. Food enters through the mouth and travels through the esophagus to the stomach. After passing through the intestines, all the useful nutrients have been extracted and all that remains is a smelly waste product.

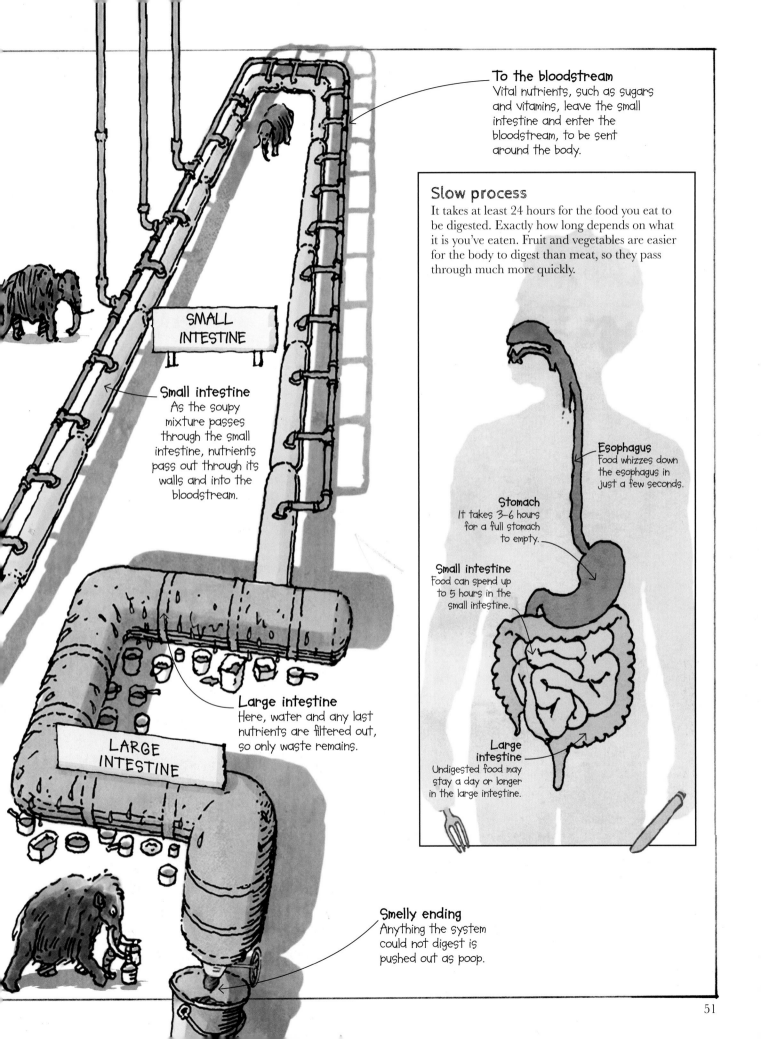

To the bloodstream
Vital nutrients, such as sugars and vitamins, leave the small intestine and enter the bloodstream, to be sent around the body.

Slow process
It takes at least 24 hours for the food you eat to be digested. Exactly how long depends on what it is you've eaten. Fruit and vegetables are easier for the body to digest than meat, so they pass through much more quickly.

SMALL INTESTINE

Small intestine
As the soupy mixture passes through the small intestine, nutrients pass out through its walls and into the bloodstream.

Esophagus
Food whizzes down the esophagus in just a few seconds.

Stomach
It takes 3–6 hours for a full stomach to empty.

Small intestine
Food can spend up to 5 hours in the small intestine.

Large intestine
Here, water and any last nutrients are filtered out, so only waste remains.

LARGE INTESTINE

Large intestine
Undigested food may stay a day or longer in the large intestine.

Smelly ending
Anything the system could not digest is pushed out as poop.

Breathing

Body cells need oxygen to work. Getting oxygen from the air into the bloodstream, so it can be delivered to body cells, is the job of the lungs. These big, spongy bags suck in air to absorb oxygen and push air back out to release waste carbon dioxide.

Taking a breath

The lungs can't move on their own—in order to breathe in, some muscle-power is needed. These mammoths are giving the lungs a helping hand, but inside your body a muscle called the diaphragm contracts to expand the lungs and suck air in from outside the body.

Breathe in ...

The diaphragm is a sheet of muscle that sits underneath the lungs. When it contracts (gets shorter), it makes the space inside the chest bigger. The intercostal muscles between the ribs help, too, by pulling the rib cage outward. The lungs expand and air rushes in.

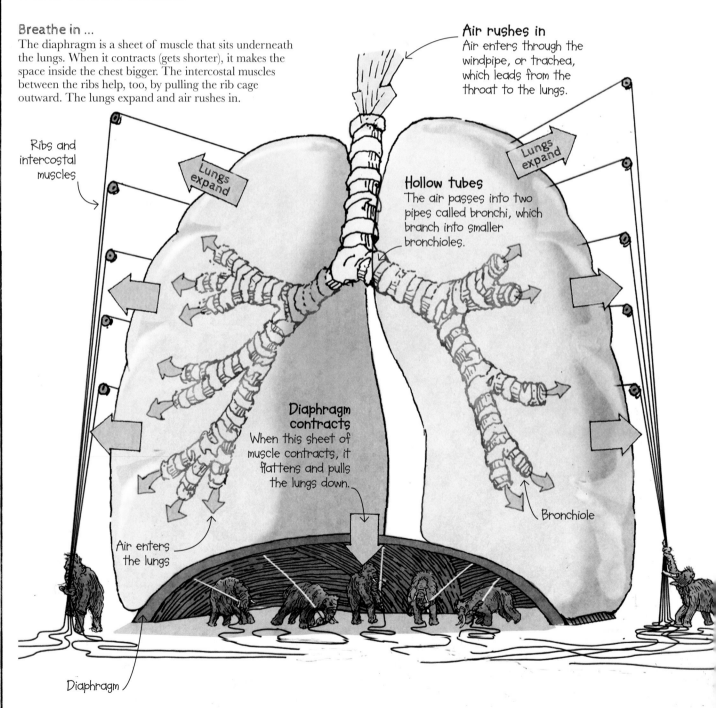

Ribs and intercostal muscles

Air rushes in
Air enters through the windpipe, or trachea, which leads from the throat to the lungs.

Lungs expand

Hollow tubes
The air passes into two pipes called bronchi, which branch into smaller bronchioles.

Lungs expand

Diaphragm contracts
When this sheet of muscle contracts, it flattens and pulls the lungs down.

Bronchiole

Air enters the lungs

Diaphragm

52

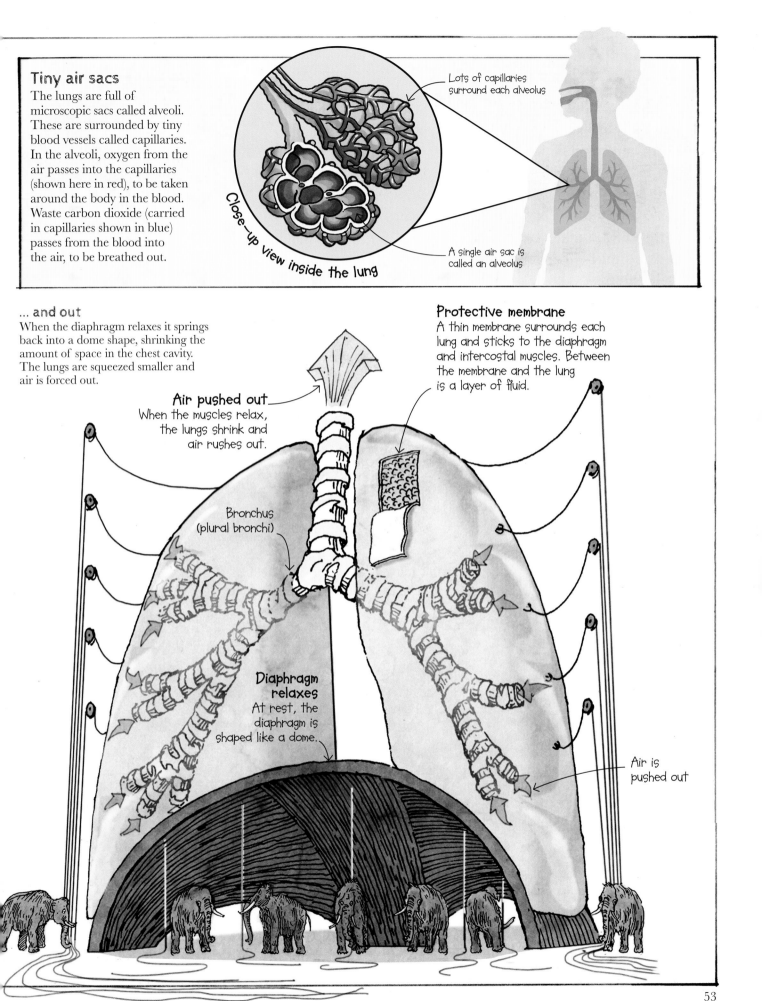

Tiny air sacs

The lungs are full of microscopic sacs called alveoli. These are surrounded by tiny blood vessels called capillaries. In the alveoli, oxygen from the air passes into the capillaries (shown here in red), to be taken around the body in the blood. Waste carbon dioxide (carried in capillaries shown in blue) passes from the blood into the air, to be breathed out.

Lots of capillaries surround each alveolus

A single air sac is called an alveolus

Close-up view inside the lung

... and out

When the diaphragm relaxes it springs back into a dome shape, shrinking the amount of space in the chest cavity. The lungs are squeezed smaller and air is forced out.

Protective membrane

A thin membrane surrounds each lung and sticks to the diaphragm and intercostal muscles. Between the membrane and the lung is a layer of fluid.

Air pushed out
When the muscles relax, the lungs shrink and air rushes out.

Bronchus (plural bronchi)

Diaphragm relaxes
At rest, the diaphragm is shaped like a dome.

Air is pushed out

Circulation

Inside you are millions of blood vessels carrying oxygen and nutrients to cells throughout your body. This incredible network is called the circulatory system. If all the blood vessels in your body were laid out, their total length could circle planet Earth twice. Just imagine how many more blood vessels are inside a massive mammoth.

Heart
This organ pumps constantly to keep blood flowing around the body.

Intricate network
Every part of the body has arteries and veins for delivering and removing blood.

Capillaries

Arteries and veins are connected by tiny vessels called capillaries. These microscopic tubes make up 98 percent of all the body's blood vessels, forming a branching network around body cells and tissues. The walls of capillaries are only one cell thick, allowing oxygen and nutrients in the bloodstream to pass into body cells, where they are used to release energy and power the cells. Waste from this process, such as carbon dioxide, seeps back into the capillaries and is carried away.

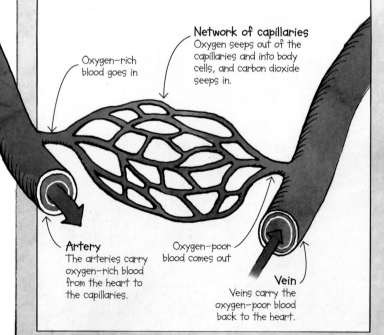

Network of capillaries
Oxygen seeps out of the capillaries and into body cells, and carbon dioxide seeps in.

Oxygen-rich blood goes in

Artery
The arteries carry oxygen-rich blood from the heart to the capillaries.

Oxygen-poor blood comes out

Vein
Veins carry the oxygen-poor blood back to the heart.

Artery
Strong vessels called arteries carry oxygen-rich blood away from the heart. Their walls are thicker because they carry blood at higher pressure than the blood in the veins.

Vein
Thin-walled veins carry oxygen-poor blood from body tissues back to the heart.

Blood network

At the center of the circulatory system is the heart. This hard-working muscle pumps blood to the lungs to collect vital oxygen, then pumps the oxygenated blood around the body. Once its oxygen cargo is delivered, blood flows back to the heart to begin the cycle again. Blood traveling away from the heart flows through muscular arteries, while blood returning from body tissues travels through thin-walled veins.

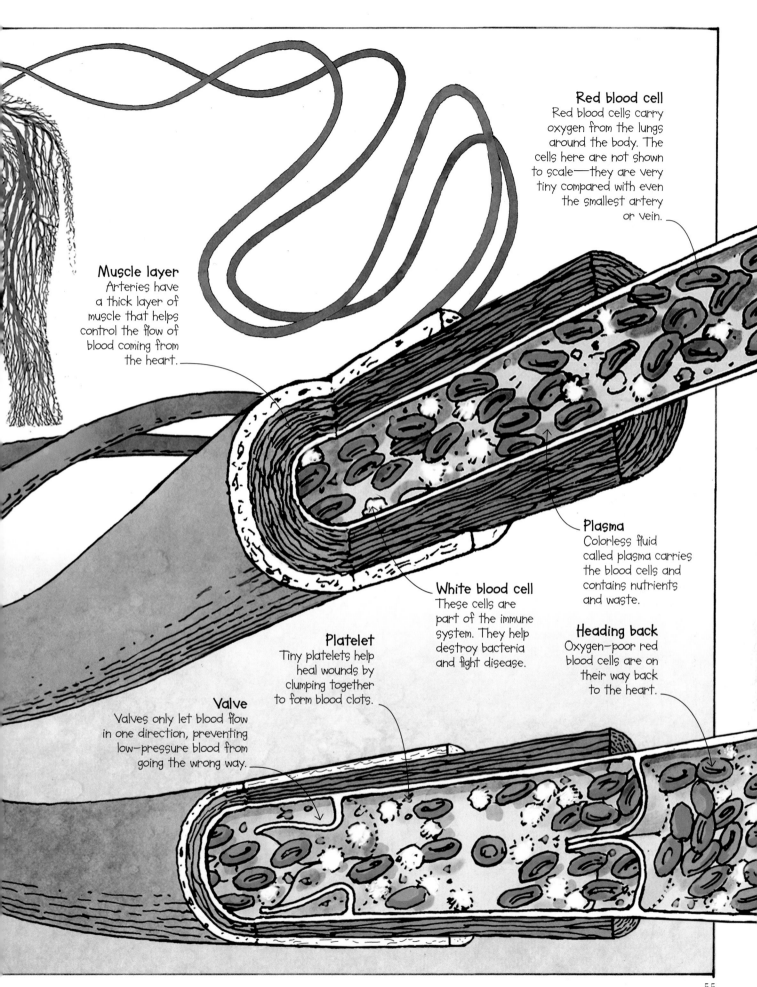

Red blood cell
Red blood cells carry oxygen from the lungs around the body. The cells here are not shown to scale—they are very tiny compared with even the smallest artery or vein.

Muscle layer
Arteries have a thick layer of muscle that helps control the flow of blood coming from the heart.

Plasma
Colorless fluid called plasma carries the blood cells and contains nutrients and waste.

White blood cell
These cells are part of the immune system. They help destroy bacteria and fight disease.

Heading back
Oxygen-poor red blood cells are on their way back to the heart.

Platelet
Tiny platelets help heal wounds by clumping together to form blood clots.

Valve
Valves only let blood flow in one direction, preventing low-pressure blood from going the wrong way.

Waste disposal

Humans and mammoths alike churn out some pretty unpleasant products. That's because cells in the body are constantly producing waste, which must be released so you can stay healthy. Waste products are flushed out of the body as urine and sweat, and breathed out when you exhale. Another type of waste is poop, which is undigested food that passes out of the digestive system.

Urinary system

The kidneys and bladder are part of the urinary system, which gets rid of waste from the bloodstream. Blood vessels carry blood to the kidneys, where harmful chemicals and excess water are removed and turned into urine. This liquid travels through two tubes called ureters to the bladder. As this storage chamber fills up, sensors alert the brain that it is time to go to the toilet. The urine leaves the body through a tube called the urethra.

Slippery sweat

If the body gets too hot, sweat is secreted by pores in the skin. Sweat contains some waste products, such as excess salt, that the body doesn't need.

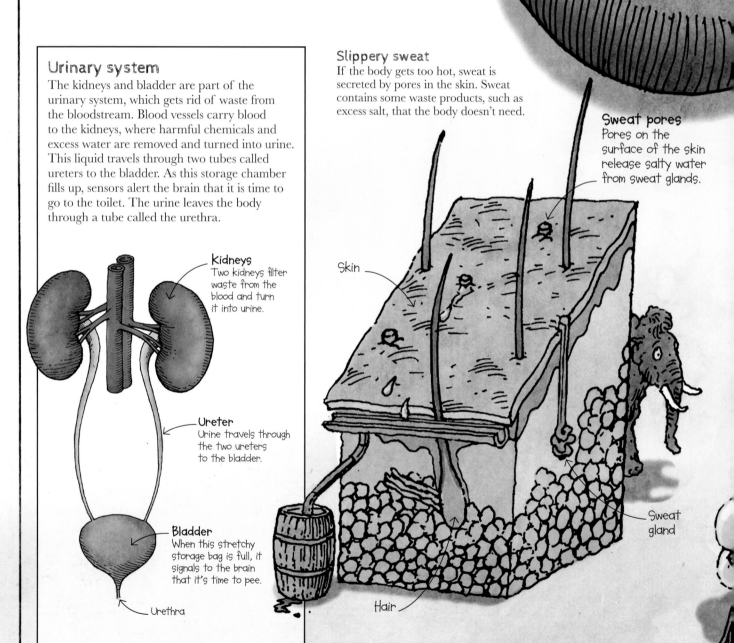

Kidneys
Two kidneys filter waste from the blood and turn it into urine.

Ureter
Urine travels through the two ureters to the bladder.

Bladder
When this stretchy storage bag is full, it signals to the brain that it's time to pee.

Urethra

Sweat pores
Pores on the surface of the skin release salty water from sweat glands.

Skin

Sweat gland

Hair

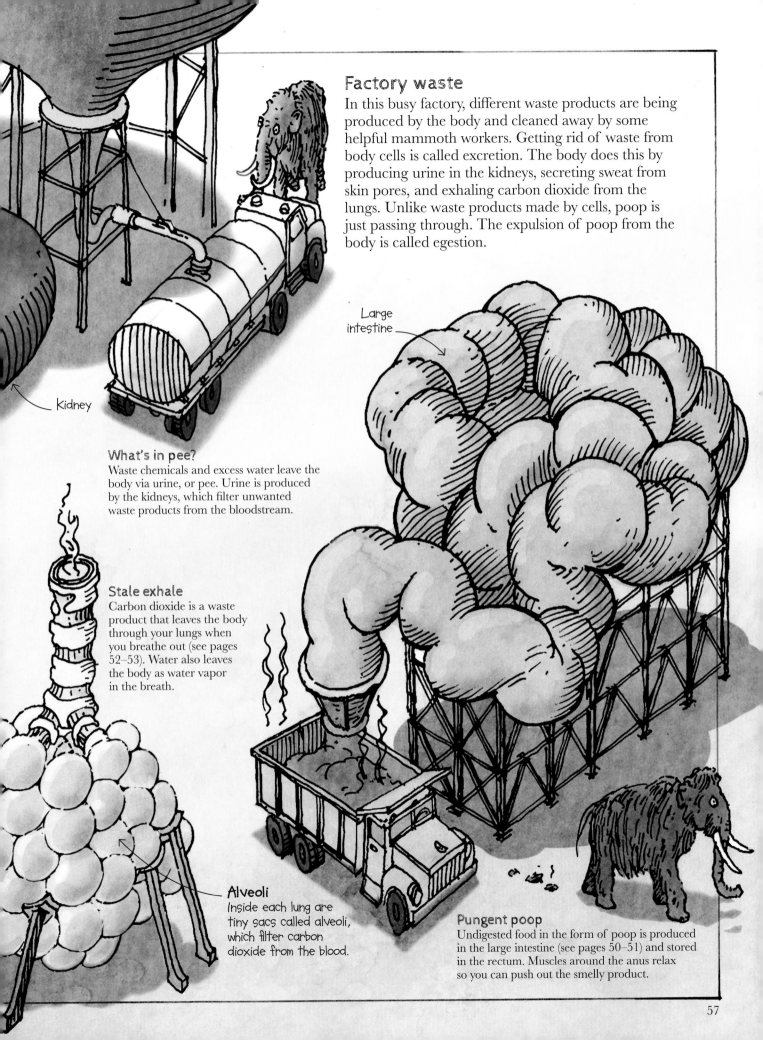

Factory waste

In this busy factory, different waste products are being produced by the body and cleaned away by some helpful mammoth workers. Getting rid of waste from body cells is called excretion. The body does this by producing urine in the kidneys, secreting sweat from skin pores, and exhaling carbon dioxide from the lungs. Unlike waste products made by cells, poop is just passing through. The expulsion of poop from the body is called egestion.

Large intestine

Kidney

What's in pee?
Waste chemicals and excess water leave the body via urine, or pee. Urine is produced by the kidneys, which filter unwanted waste products from the bloodstream.

Stale exhale
Carbon dioxide is a waste product that leaves the body through your lungs when you breathe out (see pages 52–53). Water also leaves the body as water vapor in the breath.

Alveoli
Inside each lung are tiny sacs called alveoli, which filter carbon dioxide from the blood.

Pungent poop
Undigested food in the form of poop is produced in the large intestine (see pages 50–51) and stored in the rectum. Muscles around the anus relax so you can push out the smelly product.

Bones

Masses of mighty bones lie beneath a mammoth's skin. Bones are made of tough living tissue, and join together to form a skeleton. A mammoth's bones might be a lot bigger than a human's, but they do the same job, protecting squishy inner organs like the heart and lungs, and working with the muscles and tendons to move the body around.

The skeleton

A mammoth's massive skeleton is made up of more than 300 bones. This giant X-ray machine reveals the bones in a ghostly glow. X-rays pass through soft tissues such as skin and muscle but are stopped by dense bones, so the bones show up as white shadows.

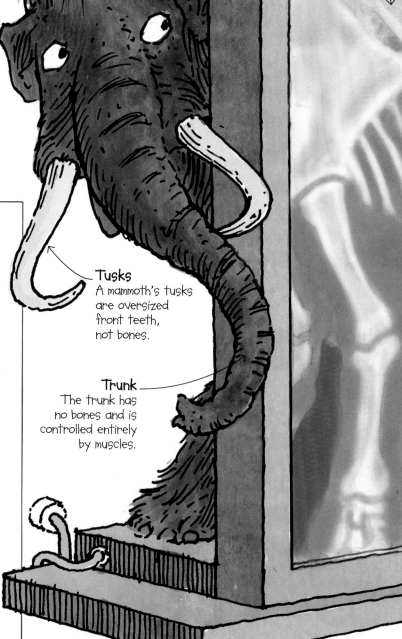

Backbone
The backbone protects the spinal cord, and is made up of many small bones called vertebrae.

Tusks
A mammoth's tusks are oversized front teeth, not bones.

Trunk
The trunk has no bones and is controlled entirely by muscles.

What's in a bone?

Bones need to be strong and hard, but they must be light, too, or we wouldn't be able to move around. Inside a bone, crisscrossing bone struts with spaces in between form a structure that is light and strong.

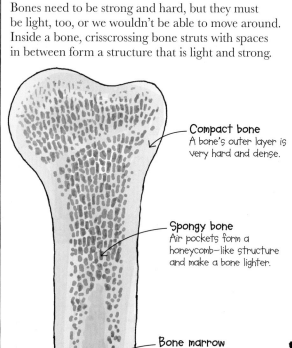

Compact bone
A bone's outer layer is very hard and dense.

Spongy bone
Air pockets form a honeycomb–like structure and make a bone lighter.

Bone marrow
Red blood cells form in the bone marrow and replace older, worn–out blood cells.

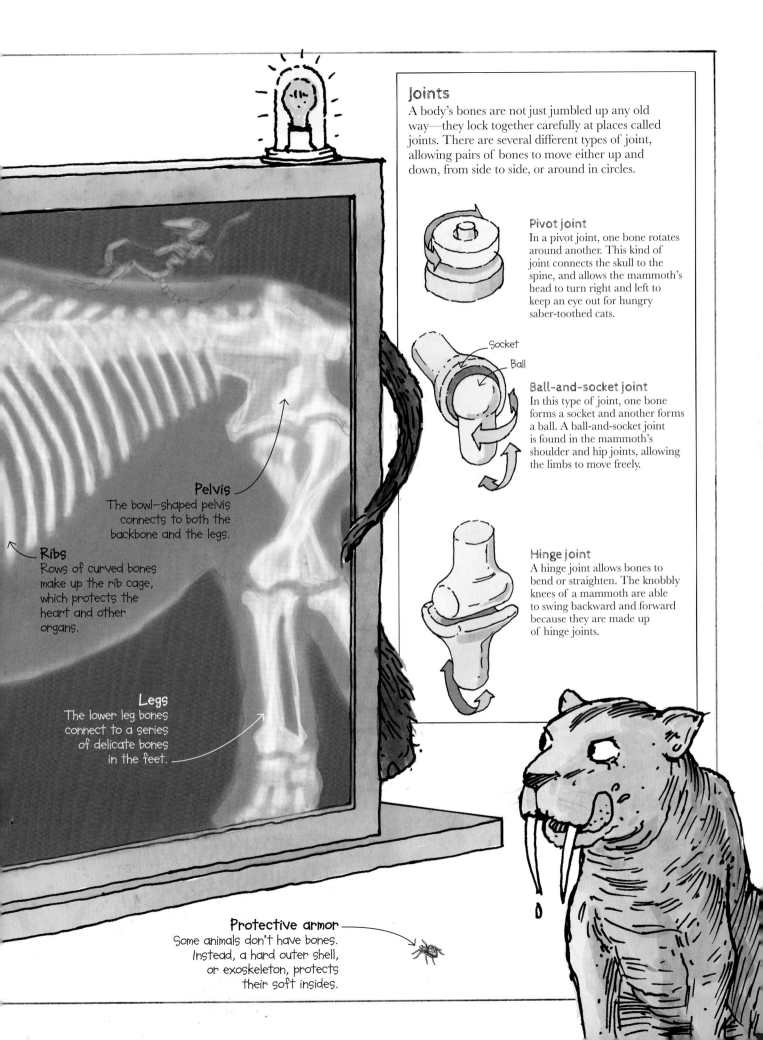

Joints

A body's bones are not just jumbled up any old way—they lock together carefully at places called joints. There are several different types of joint, allowing pairs of bones to move either up and down, from side to side, or around in circles.

Pivot joint
In a pivot joint, one bone rotates around another. This kind of joint connects the skull to the spine, and allows the mammoth's head to turn right and left to keep an eye out for hungry saber-toothed cats.

Socket
Ball

Ball-and-socket joint
In this type of joint, one bone forms a socket and another forms a ball. A ball-and-socket joint is found in the mammoth's shoulder and hip joints, allowing the limbs to move freely.

Hinge joint
A hinge joint allows bones to bend or straighten. The knobbly knees of a mammoth are able to swing backward and forward because they are made up of hinge joints.

Pelvis
The bowl-shaped pelvis connects to both the backbone and the legs.

Ribs
Rows of curved bones make up the rib cage, which protects the heart and other organs.

Legs
The lower leg bones connect to a series of delicate bones in the feet.

Protective armor
Some animals don't have bones. Instead, a hard outer shell, or exoskeleton, protects their soft insides.

Muscles

A strong skeleton wouldn't be much use without muscles to move it around. These bundles of tissue contract (shorten) to pull on bones, making them move. The human body has more than 650 muscles and many of these work together in pairs. These mammoths are getting a work out demonstrating the pair of muscles found in the human upper arm—the biceps and triceps.

Muscle pairs

Muscles work by contracting—squeezing their fibers to get shorter. This means they can only pull, not push, so for joints to move in two different directions muscles work in pairs. One muscle contracts to pull the bone one way, then the other contracts to move the bone back.

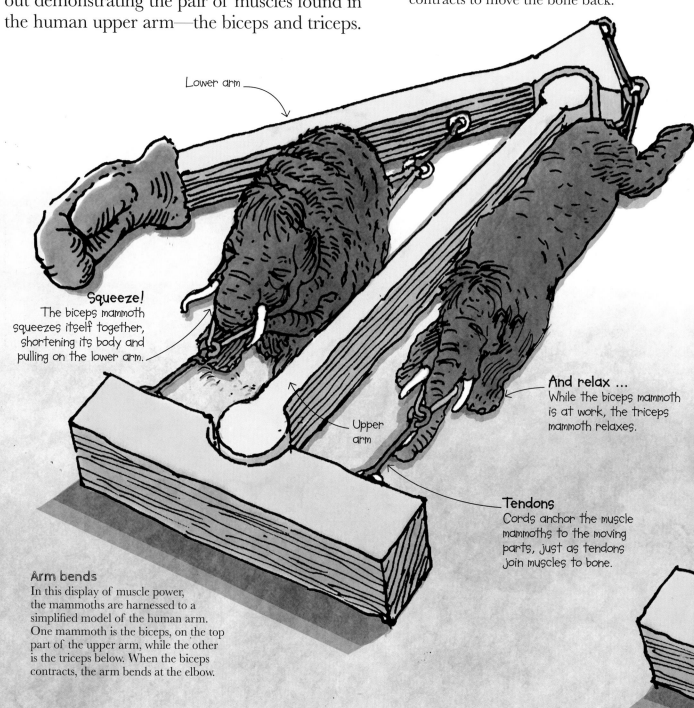

Lower arm

Squeeze!
The biceps mammoth squeezes itself together, shortening its body and pulling on the lower arm.

Upper arm

And relax ...
While the biceps mammoth is at work, the triceps mammoth relaxes.

Tendons
Cords anchor the muscle mammoths to the moving parts, just as tendons join muscles to bone.

Arm bends
In this display of muscle power, the mammoths are harnessed to a simplified model of the human arm. One mammoth is the biceps, on the top part of the upper arm, while the other is the triceps below. When the biceps contracts, the arm bends at the elbow.

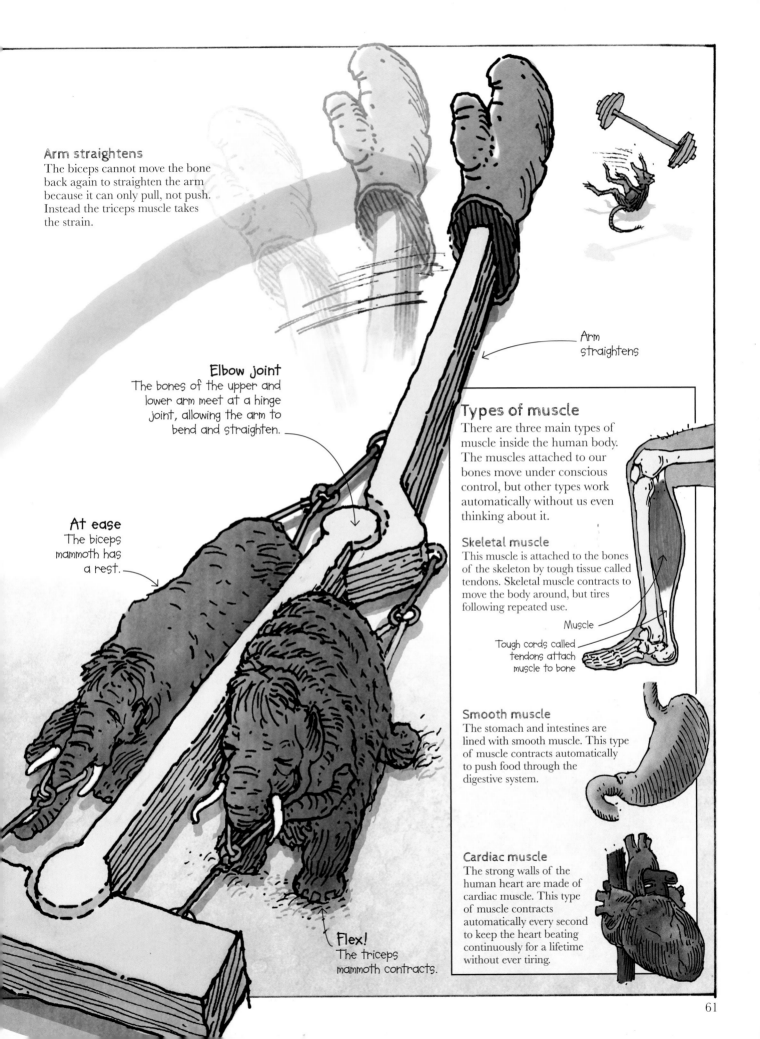

Arm straightens
The biceps cannot move the bone back again to straighten the arm because it can only pull, not push. Instead the triceps muscle takes the strain.

Arm straightens

Elbow joint
The bones of the upper and lower arm meet at a hinge joint, allowing the arm to bend and straighten.

At ease
The biceps mammoth has a rest.

Types of muscle
There are three main types of muscle inside the human body. The muscles attached to our bones move under conscious control, but other types work automatically without us even thinking about it.

Skeletal muscle
This muscle is attached to the bones of the skeleton by tough tissue called tendons. Skeletal muscle contracts to move the body around, but tires following repeated use.

Muscle

Tough cords called tendons attach muscle to bone

Smooth muscle
The stomach and intestines are lined with smooth muscle. This type of muscle contracts automatically to push food through the digestive system.

Flex!
The triceps mammoth contracts.

Cardiac muscle
The strong walls of the human heart are made of cardiac muscle. This type of muscle contracts automatically every second to keep the heart beating continuously for a lifetime without ever tiring.

Nervous system

Animals can sense and respond to things around them as quick as a flash because their bodies are controlled by their nervous system. Billions of interconnecting nerve cells, called neurons, make up this super-speedy communications network, carrying messages as electrical nerve impulses around the body quicker than the blink of an eye.

Control and communication

The human nervous system has two parts: the central nervous system (CNS), made up of the brain and spinal cord, and the peripheral nervous system, which carries signals throughout the body on a network of nerves. Sensory nerves send information as signals to the brain from the sense receptors, while motor nerves send instructions as signals from the brain to muscles and organs.

Brain
The brain is made up of billions of neurons and controls almost all the body's activities.

Spinal cord
Connecting the brain to the rest of the body, the spinal cord is a thick thread of neurons about the width of a finger.

Nerves
The nerves reach every part of the body. They are made from neurons that have long branching fibers to transmit signals.

Sensing and reacting

The nervous system controls many processes, such as breathing and digestion, without the body even being aware of it. But some responses are consciously controlled: when this mammoth spots a hungry predator lurking in the undergrowth, the nervous system is fired into action.

Scary sight
The hungry saber-toothed cat suddenly appears from behind the bushes.

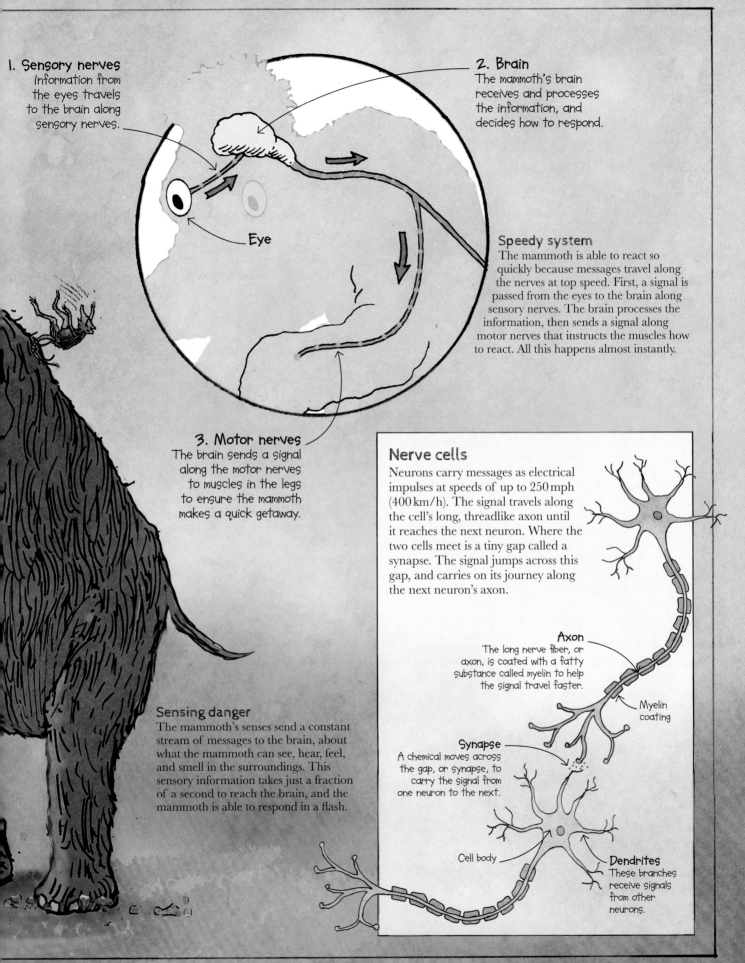

1. Sensory nerves
Information from the eyes travels to the brain along sensory nerves.

2. Brain
The mammoth's brain receives and processes the information, and decides how to respond.

Eye

Speedy system
The mammoth is able to react so quickly because messages travel along the nerves at top speed. First, a signal is passed from the eyes to the brain along sensory nerves. The brain processes the information, then sends a signal along motor nerves that instructs the muscles how to react. All this happens almost instantly.

3. Motor nerves
The brain sends a signal along the motor nerves to muscles in the legs to ensure the mammoth makes a quick getaway.

Nerve cells
Neurons carry messages as electrical impulses at speeds of up to 250 mph (400 km/h). The signal travels along the cell's long, threadlike axon until it reaches the next neuron. Where the two cells meet is a tiny gap called a synapse. The signal jumps across this gap, and carries on its journey along the next neuron's axon.

Axon
The long nerve fiber, or axon, is coated with a fatty substance called myelin to help the signal travel faster.

Myelin coating

Synapse
A chemical moves across the gap, or synapse, to carry the signal from one neuron to the next.

Sensing danger
The mammoth's senses send a constant stream of messages to the brain, about what the mammoth can see, hear, feel, and smell in the surroundings. This sensory information takes just a fraction of a second to reach the brain, and the mammoth is able to respond in a flash.

Cell body

Dendrites
These branches receive signals from other neurons.

The eye

The eye is an amazing organ. It captures light from our surroundings to give the brain a clear picture of what's around us. From tiny elephant shrews to humans to huge, hairy mammoths, all mammals have eyes that work the same way. Light enters through a hole called the pupil and is focused onto the light-sensitive retina.

Inside the eye

This cross-section view shows how the eye detects an image. Light enters the eye and passes through a clear disk called the lens. The lens bends the light (see page 91) to focus a sharp, upside-down image on the retina at the back of the eye. Light-sensitive cells on the retina convert the image to nerve impulses and send them to the brain, which processes the image, flipping it the right way up.

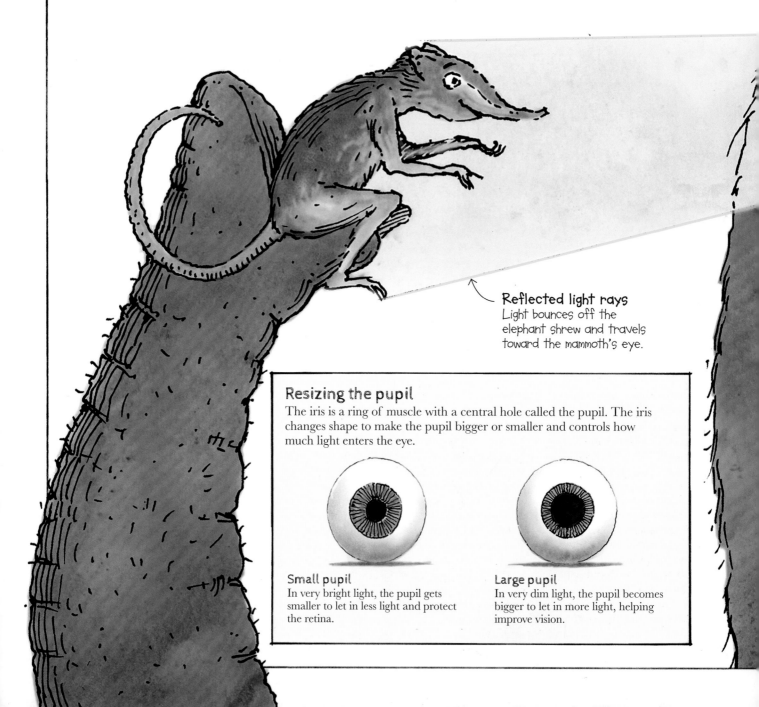

Reflected light rays
Light bounces off the elephant shrew and travels toward the mammoth's eye.

Resizing the pupil

The iris is a ring of muscle with a central hole called the pupil. The iris changes shape to make the pupil bigger or smaller and controls how much light enters the eye.

Small pupil
In very bright light, the pupil gets smaller to let in less light and protect the retina.

Large pupil
In very dim light, the pupil becomes bigger to let in more light, helping improve vision.

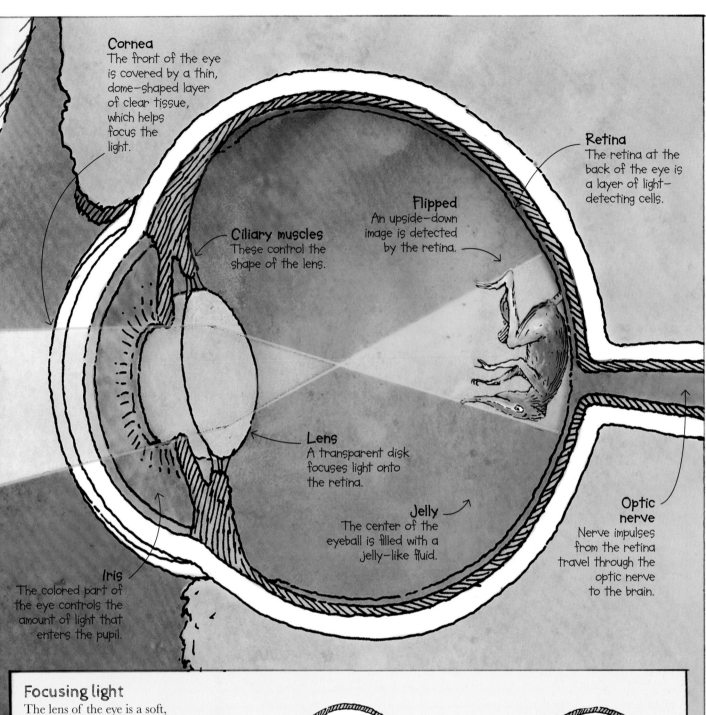

Cornea
The front of the eye is covered by a thin, dome-shaped layer of clear tissue, which helps focus the light.

Ciliary muscles
These control the shape of the lens.

Flipped
An upside-down image is detected by the retina.

Retina
The retina at the back of the eye is a layer of light-detecting cells.

Lens
A transparent disk focuses light onto the retina.

Jelly
The center of the eyeball is filled with a jelly-like fluid.

Optic nerve
Nerve impulses from the retina travel through the optic nerve to the brain.

Iris
The colored part of the eye controls the amount of light that enters the pupil.

Focusing light

The lens of the eye is a soft, transparent disk that focuses light onto the retina. In order to clearly see objects at different distances, the lens has to change shape. The ciliary muscles attached to the lens automatically relax and contract, pulling the lens thin to focus light from distant objects or widening it to focus light from near objects. The muscles are constantly making adjustments to fine-tune the focus.

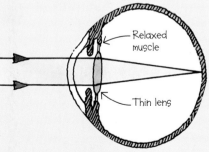

Relaxed muscle

Thin lens

Distant focus
To focus on distant objects, the muscles relax, which pulls the lens thinner. This makes distant objects clear and close objects blurred.

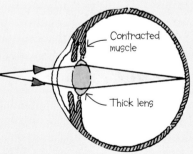

Contracted muscle

Thick lens

Near focus
To focus on closer objects, the muscles contract and the lens widens. Close objects are sharp and distant objects are blurred.

The ear

Mammoth ears are much larger than ours, but they work in the same way—converting sound waves into information that the brain can understand. Large, furry flaps on the sides of the head are just the entrance to the ear. The hard work is all happening inside.

How we hear

Sound waves enter the ear canal and are picked up by the eardrum. The vibrations are then amplified by the three tiny ossicle bones in the middle ear before they move into the inner ear and through the cochlea. The cochlea translates the vibrations into nerve impulses, which are carried to the brain by the auditory nerve.

Ear canal
A tube-like passage carries sound waves from the outer ear to the middle ear.

Pinna
The outer part of the ear collects sound waves and channels them into the ear canal.

Outer ear

HOW TO MAKE SHREWD INVESTMENTS

Sensing movement

The semicircular canals in the inner ear are filled with fluid. When the head moves, the fluid moves, sending nerve impulses to the brain. This helps the brain figure out the body's position and stops you from falling over.

Spinning
When fluid in the semicircular canals spins, the brain knows the head is turning.

Stationary
No movement of fluid in the semicircular canals means the head isn't moving.

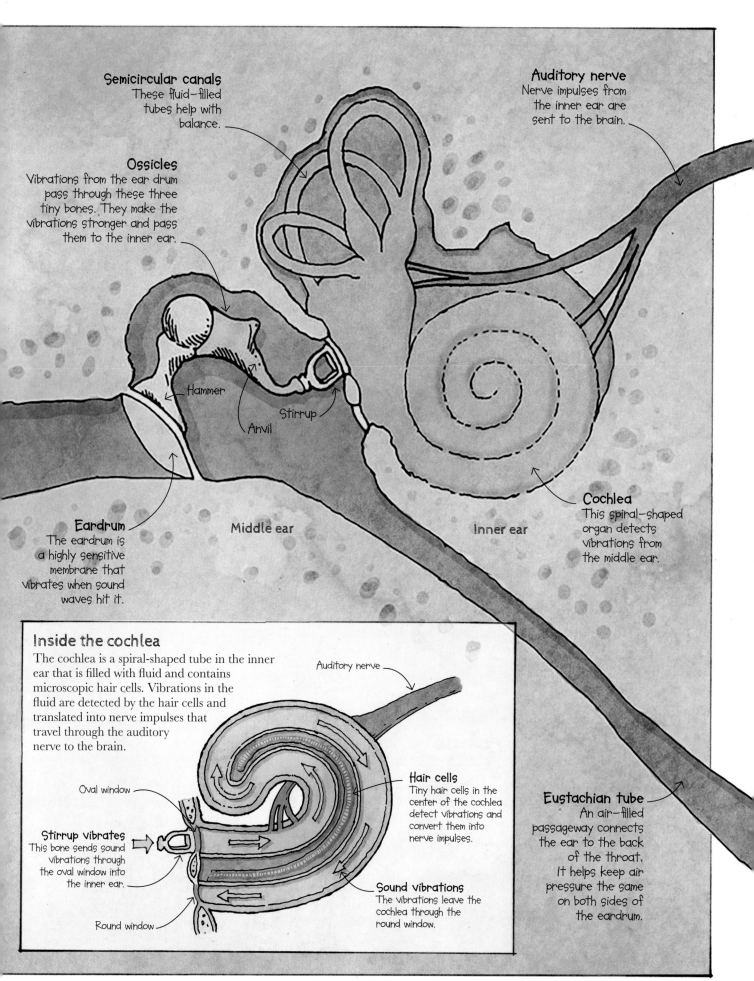

Semicircular canals
These fluid–filled tubes help with balance.

Ossicles
Vibrations from the ear drum pass through these three tiny bones. They make the vibrations stronger and pass them to the inner ear.

Auditory nerve
Nerve impulses from the inner ear are sent to the brain.

Hammer

Anvil

Stirrup

Eardrum
The eardrum is a highly sensitive membrane that vibrates when sound waves hit it.

Middle ear

Inner ear

Cochlea
This spiral–shaped organ detects vibrations from the middle ear.

Inside the cochlea

The cochlea is a spiral-shaped tube in the inner ear that is filled with fluid and contains microscopic hair cells. Vibrations in the fluid are detected by the hair cells and translated into nerve impulses that travel through the auditory nerve to the brain.

Auditory nerve

Oval window

Stirrup vibrates
This bone sends sound vibrations through the oval window into the inner ear.

Round window

Hair cells
Tiny hair cells in the center of the cochlea detect vibrations and convert them into nerve impulses.

Sound vibrations
The vibrations leave the cochlea through the round window.

Eustachian tube
An air–filled passageway connects the ear to the back of the throat. It helps keep air pressure the same on both sides of the eardrum.

Body defenses

The body is constantly under attack from germs—harmful microbes such as bacteria and viruses. Luckily, there are lots of barriers to prevent an enemy invasion. Skin is the body's first line of defense, forming a wall stopping germs from entering. Inside the body, saliva, tears, and mucus help wash away any invaders. If these fluid defenses fail, the body's immune system sends armies of soldierlike cells to target and kill the enemy, restoring the body to full health.

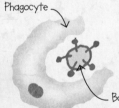

Renew and rebuild
If the skin is damaged it is repaired, just like this wall. Tiny cells in the blood called platelets clot together to form a scab. This stops bacteria getting in while the skin heals.

The immune system

The body's barriers are very effective but they can't keep out all invaders. The immune system fights germs that have entered the body, and builds immunity against future infection. It does this by identifying invading germs and producing chemicals called antibodies that target them.

Phagocyte

1. First response
White blood cells called phagocytes surround and swallow up invading bacteria, destroying them.

Bacterium

2. Identify
Another kind of white blood cell called a lymphocyte identifies the bacteria and produces antibodies to combat them.

Lymphocyte

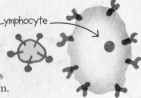

Antibodies

3. Fighting back
When the same bacteria invade in future, trillions of antibodies are released to fight the infection.

Window wipers
Salty tears wash away dirt from the eyeballs. Tears contain a chemical that helps kill bacteria.

Mammoth fortress
The body of a mighty mammoth is like a giant fortress designed to stop invaders from entering. The attackers here are elephant shrews, but the body is fighting much smaller foes—microscopic bacteria and viruses.

Attack!
The elephant shrews attacking the fortress are playing the role of invading germs.

Slippery saliva
The fortress moat is like the slimy saliva that keeps the mouth moist and clean. Saliva contains bacteria-killing chemicals.

Gloppy mucus
The shrews are stuck in this sticky mucus. The mucus that lines the nose (or trunk) traps dust, bacteria, or viruses inhaled through the nostrils.

Outer barrier
The skin is the body's fortress wall. It is a physical barrier against invading bacteria and germs.

Growing up

All living things grow and change. An animal's progress from birth to adulthood is called its life cycle. Young animals often look a lot like miniature versions of their parents, but their bodies undergo important changes as they get older.

Getting bigger
The mammoth gets bigger and taller and grows tusks.

Baby body
Baby mammals have bigger heads and shorter legs, in proportion to their body size, than adults do.

Infancy
A newly born mammal depends on its parents for food and protection. Its body grows rapidly, but the young animal is also developing mentally—learning about the world around it and how to survive.

Youth
Growth slows down but the young animal is still developing. It learns to become more independent of its parents, finding food and looking out for dangers.

Metamorphosis

Mammals get bigger as they grow into adults, but some animals change their body shape and way of life entirely. This dramatic transformation is called metamorphosis. The change is so extreme that the same creature is unrecognizable at different stages of life, like the beautiful butterfly that begins life as a creeping caterpillar.

Egg
Butterflies lay their tiny eggs on the underside of leaves, where they cannot be seen.

Caterpillar
A caterpillar hatches from the egg and immediately starts to eat. It continues to eat and grow.

Chrysalis
Once it has stopped growing, the caterpillar develops a hard case called a chrysalis.

Butterfly
Inside the case, the caterpillar is transformed. In a few weeks, it will emerge as a butterfly.

Prime of life
This adult mammoth has reached its full size and strength.

Stages of life
A baby mammoth has a lot of growing up to do. Like all mammals, including humans, mammoths start small and get bigger, until they reach adulthood and become sexually mature—able to produce offspring of their own.

Winding down
As the body loses muscle tissue, the mammoth shrinks in height.

Fully grown
In adulthood, the body reaches its full height and strength, and bones stop growing. The body has reached sexual maturity and is able to produce offspring, so the life cycle can start all over again.

Old age
In old age, bones and muscles weaken and joints begin to stiffen. The skin loses its stretchiness and starts to sag. Eyesight and hearing may fail. The mammoth is reaching the end of its life cycle.

Making mammals
Mammoths, elephant shrews, and humans are all placental mammals. Their babies grow inside the mother's body, supported by an organ called the placenta, until they are ready to be born.

Single offspring
Most large mammals have just one baby at a time.

Large litter
Smaller mammals tend to give birth to more young at a time.

Mother's milk
Female mammals produce nutritious milk to feed their babies.

Reproduction

What do you get if you cross a male mammoth with a female mammoth? A mini mammoth! All fully grown living things have a way to reproduce themselves—without this, species would die out and life could not exist. Most animals create new life by combining cells from two parents, in a process called sexual reproduction.

New life

Sexual reproduction needs two parents: a male and a female. Each parent produces special cells called sex cells, which have half the usual number of chromosomes (see page 74). These sex cells can combine and grow into a new organism, which will have a mixture of chromosomes inherited from both parents. This means that in sexual reproduction each new organism is unique.

How an embryo develops

Male sex cells are called sperm and female sex cells are called eggs. When two sex cells join, they make a new cell, which grows into an embryo. In mammals, this happens inside the female's body, and the developing embryo is supported by an organ called the placenta.

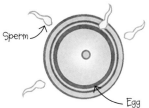

Sperm

Egg

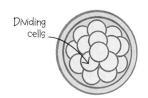

Dividing cells

1 Fertilization
The first sperm to reach the egg burrows through the outer case of the egg. The two cells join together in a process known as fertilization.

2 Cell divides
Within a few hours, the new cell begins to divide, and goes on dividing until it has formed a tiny ball of cells called an embryo.

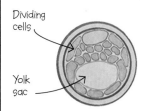

Dividing cells

Yolk sac

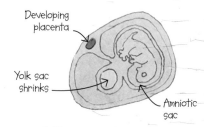

Developing placenta

Yolk sac shrinks

Amniotic sac

3 Embryo implants
The embryo continues to grow, nourished by a temporary yolk sac, and attaches itself to the lining of the mother's uterus.

4 Placenta takes over
An organ called the placenta then develops to supply food and oxygen, and remove waste. The fluid-filled amniotic sac protects the embryo.

Laying eggs

All birds and most insects, reptiles, and fish lay eggs. The embryo develops inside until it is ready to hatch. Then the baby animal breaks through the shell or membrane and flops, wriggles, or swims into the world.

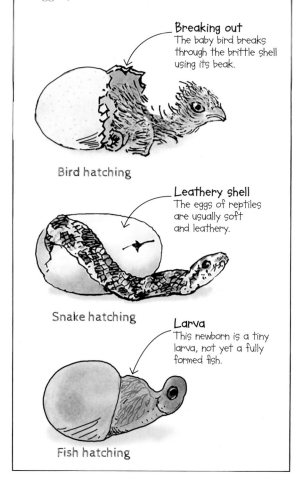

Breaking out
The baby bird breaks through the brittle shell using its beak.

Bird hatching

Leathery shell
The eggs of reptiles are usually soft and leathery.

Snake hatching

Larva
This newborn is a tiny larva, not yet a fully formed fish.

Fish hatching

Producing clones

Some animals can reproduce themselves on their own, without a mate. This is called asexual reproduction. The offspring produced are identical copies, or clones, of their parent because they share exactly the same set of genes. Aphids are tiny insects that can reproduce in this way to generate huge numbers of young in a short space of time.

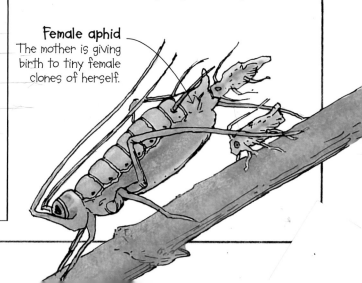

Female aphid
The mother is giving birth to tiny female clones of herself.

DNA

All the instructions needed to make a living organism are stored in a big molecule with a very long name: deoxyribonucleic acid, or DNA for short. DNA is found inside the cells of all living things, packed into bundles called chromosomes. If you could unravel a chromosome you'd see the distinctive twisted ladder shape of the DNA molecule itself, known as the double helix.

Chromosome
Chromosomes are found inside the cell nucleus. Humans have 46 chromosomes.

Histone
DNA coils around a simple ball-shaped protein called histone to help pack itself up inside the chromosome.

Base pairs
Just four chemicals form the "rungs" of the ladder. Each base can only pair with one other.

Gene
A gene is a stretch of DNA. The order of the bases in that particular stretch contains a single instruction.

The long sides are called the backbone

Identical twins

Every individual has a unique set of genes, except for identical twins. Identical twins have the same DNA, which determines many of their physical characteristics, such as eye color and hair color. However, not all characteristics are entirely decided by genes. Some are influenced by environment or lifestyle. For example, your height is determined partly by your genes and partly by other factors such as diet.

Identical genes
Identical twins inherit exactly the same genes from their parents.

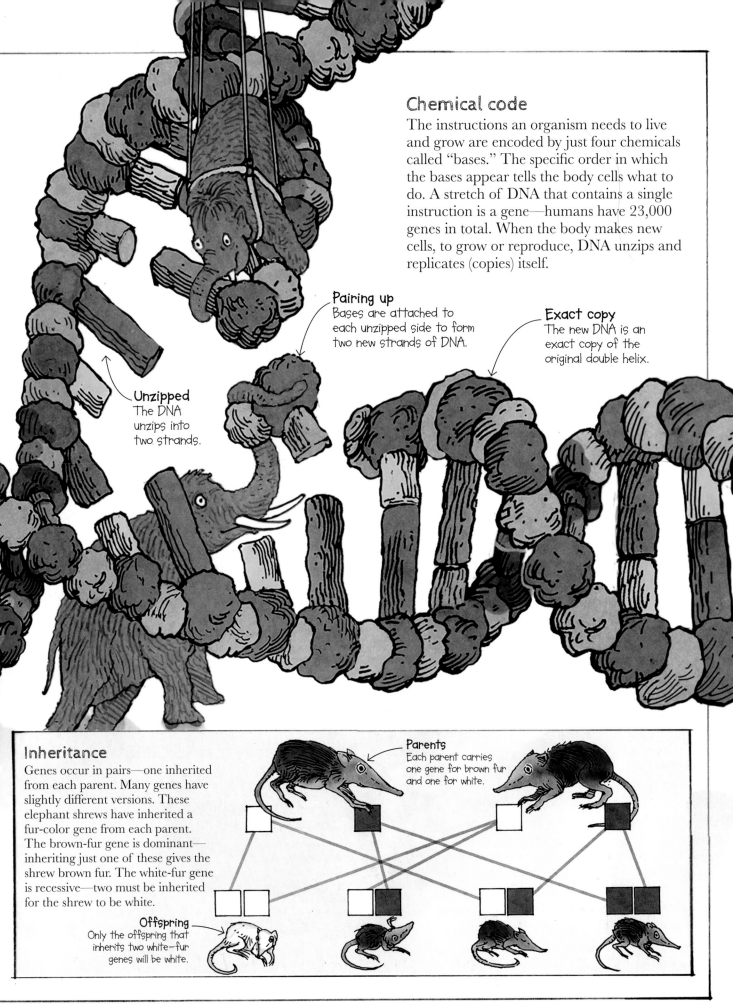

Chemical code

The instructions an organism needs to live and grow are encoded by just four chemicals called "bases." The specific order in which the bases appear tells the body cells what to do. A stretch of DNA that contains a single instruction is a gene—humans have 23,000 genes in total. When the body makes new cells, to grow or reproduce, DNA unzips and replicates (copies) itself.

Pairing up
Bases are attached to each unzipped side to form two new strands of DNA.

Exact copy
The new DNA is an exact copy of the original double helix.

Unzipped
The DNA unzips into two strands.

Inheritance

Genes occur in pairs—one inherited from each parent. Many genes have slightly different versions. These elephant shrews have inherited a fur-color gene from each parent. The brown-fur gene is dominant—inheriting just one of these gives the shrew brown fur. The white-fur gene is recessive—two must be inherited for the shrew to be white.

Parents
Each parent carries one gene for brown fur and one for white.

Offspring
Only the offspring that inherits two white-fur genes will be white.

Evolution

Life on Earth has not always looked the way it does today. Over millions of years, species change as they adapt to their environment—new species come into being, and other ones die out. This long process of change over time is called evolution.

Mobile trunk
Primelephas's long trunk was possibly used for grasping food in the woodlands where it lived.

Paleomastodon
This early elephant relative lived about 28 million years ago. It had a short trunk, short tusks, and ears set far back on its head.

Gomphotherium
Gomphotherium had bigger tusks—two pointy ones in its upper jaw and two flatter, shovel-shaped ones in its lower jaw. It walked the Earth about 10 million years ago.

Primelephas
This animal had longer upper tusks and shorter lower ones than its relative Gomphotherium, and lived 6 million years ago. Closely related to mammoths and modern elephants, its name means "first elephant."

Meet the family

Evolution happens over countless generations and produces new kinds of animals. Our woolly mammoth is part of a great family tree of species that includes animals that lived in the distant past, and two—the African and Asian elephants—that are still around today.

Natural selection

The driving force of evolution is natural selection. Organisms that are more suited to their environment survive, and pass on their winning features to future generations. The green beetles on this tree stand out and are picked off by the birds. But the brown beetles survive. Eventually most of the beetles of this species will be brown.

Brown beetles are less visible

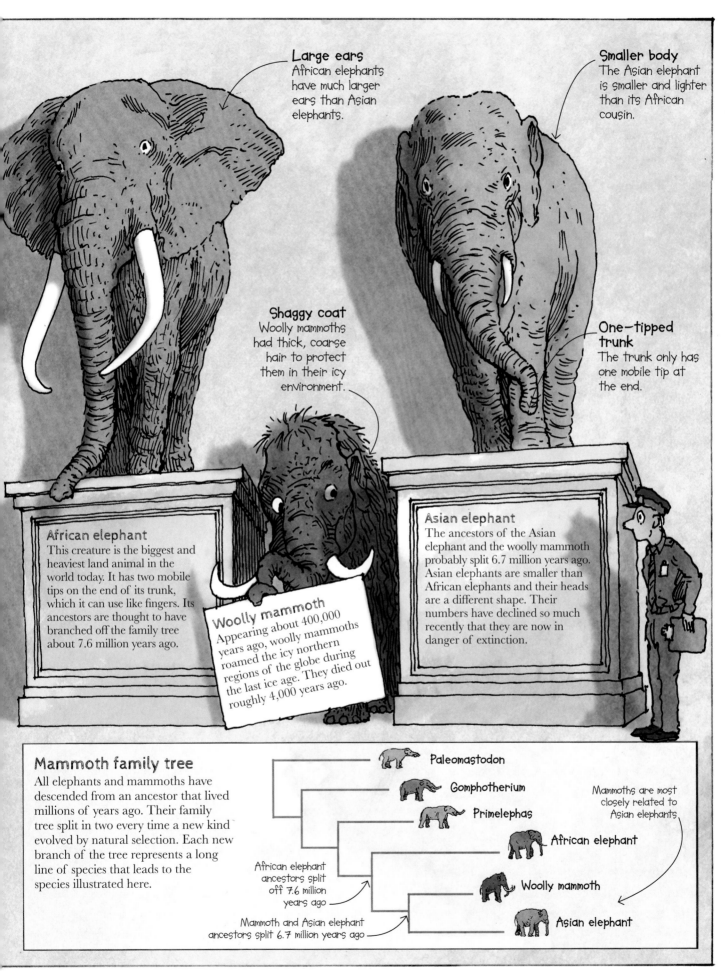

Large ears
African elephants have much larger ears than Asian elephants.

Smaller body
The Asian elephant is smaller and lighter than its African cousin.

Shaggy coat
Woolly mammoths had thick, coarse hair to protect them in their icy environment.

One-tipped trunk
The trunk only has one mobile tip at the end.

African elephant
This creature is the biggest and heaviest land animal in the world today. It has two mobile tips on the end of its trunk, which it can use like fingers. Its ancestors are thought to have branched off the family tree about 7.6 million years ago.

Woolly mammoth
Appearing about 400,000 years ago, woolly mammoths roamed the icy northern regions of the globe during the last ice age. They died out roughly 4,000 years ago.

Asian elephant
The ancestors of the Asian elephant and the woolly mammoth probably split 6.7 million years ago. Asian elephants are smaller than African elephants and their heads are a different shape. Their numbers have declined so much recently that they are now in danger of extinction.

Mammoth family tree
All elephants and mammoths have descended from an ancestor that lived millions of years ago. Their family tree split in two every time a new kind evolved by natural selection. Each new branch of the tree represents a long line of species that leads to the species illustrated here.

Paleomastodon

Gomphotherium

Primelephas

African elephant

Woolly mammoth

Asian elephant

Mammoths are most closely related to Asian elephants.

African elephant ancestors split off 7.6 million years ago

Mammoth and Asian elephant ancestors split 6.7 million years ago

Energy

What is energy?

Everything that happens in the universe, from the sun shining to you reading this book right now, uses energy. Energy is what makes everything go, and it is all around us all the time. Energy can't be created or destroyed, but it can be stored and transferred in different ways.

1. At the top
Energy stored so it can be used later is called potential energy. Sitting on the high platform, the mammoth has stored gravitational potential energy. This is energy that can be transferred when gravity pulls the mammoth back to Earth.

Falling
Potential energy transfers to kinetic energy as the mammoth falls.

2. Jumping down
When the mammoth jumps off the platform, it falls downward, gaining speed. Energy possessed by moving objects is called kinetic energy: the heavier something is and the faster it moves, the more kinetic energy it has.

Loud landing
When the mammoth hits the ground, some energy is transferred to the surroundings by heat and sound.

3. Squashed springs
The springs on the mammoth's feet store energy when they are squashed. When the mammoth lands, most of its kinetic energy is transferred to the springs. Some of the energy is transferred by sound—the noise the mammoth's body makes when it crashes to the ground.

Energy transfers

It's easy to see how energy is at work when you flick a light switch or ride a bicycle. But there are lots of less obvious ways in which energy is stored and transferred. This daring stunt mammoth has climbed a high platform. Anything raised off the ground has the potential to fall back down again, so we say the mammoth has a store of potential energy. When the mammoth takes a leap, the potential energy is transferred into motion.

4. Bouncing back

When the springs uncoil, they release their elastic energy, which is transferred to kinetic energy again as the mammoth flies into the air. This daredevil might keep bouncing, but each bounce will be smaller than the last, as each time some energy is transferred as heat and sound.

Energy around us

All energy is really the same, but to make it easier to understand we talk about the different ways energy is stored or used in the world around us. This makes it easier to describe how energy is transferred and makes things happen. For example, the energy stored in the chemicals inside a battery can be transferred to other objects by electricity. Light bulbs and buzzers can then transfer that energy by light, heat, or sound.

Kinetic energy
The energy stored in moving objects, whether mammoths or balls.

Light
A way of transferring energy that our eyes can detect.

Sound
Energy transferred through solids, liquids, or gases by vibrations.

Heat energy
Energy that is stored in hot objects and transferred to others by heating.

Elastic energy
Potential energy that is stored in a coiled spring.

Nuclear energy
The energy stored inside atoms.

Chemical energy
Energy stored by chemical compounds.

Electrical energy
The transfer of energy by moving charges.

Heat

How hot or cold something is depends on how fast its particles are moving—the faster they move, the hotter they are. Heat is energy that makes the particles move faster, raising an object's temperature. Heat can be transferred from one thing to another and always travels from hot areas to colder ones, as these elephant shrews are finding out.

Heat transfer

By holding a metal bar to a flame, the mammoth is making the elephant shrews hot under the collar. Heat is transferred along the bar by conduction. The particles in the solid bar are not free to move around, but they vibrate more, bumping into one another and passing on their energy. There are two other ways in which heat can be transferred. Hot objects transfer heat by radiation—sending out invisible rays called infrared through the air (see pages 96–97). In liquids and gases, heat is transferred by convection.

High energy
The end of the metal bar is heated by the flame, making its particles vibrate rapidly.

Gaining energy
As the particles of the metal knock into each other, energy passes from the hottest part of the bar to cooler parts.

Red hot
The hot metal bar gives off invisible rays called infrared radiation, and the hottest parts emit red or yellow light.

Heat and temperature
An object's temperature is how hot or cold it is. But how much heat energy something has also depends on its mass. Objects with more mass store more heat energy. There is more heat energy stored in a freezing cold iceberg than there is in a piping hot cup of tea. This is because although the iceberg's particles are not moving as fast, there are far more of them.

Huge, cold iceberg

Small, hot cup of tea

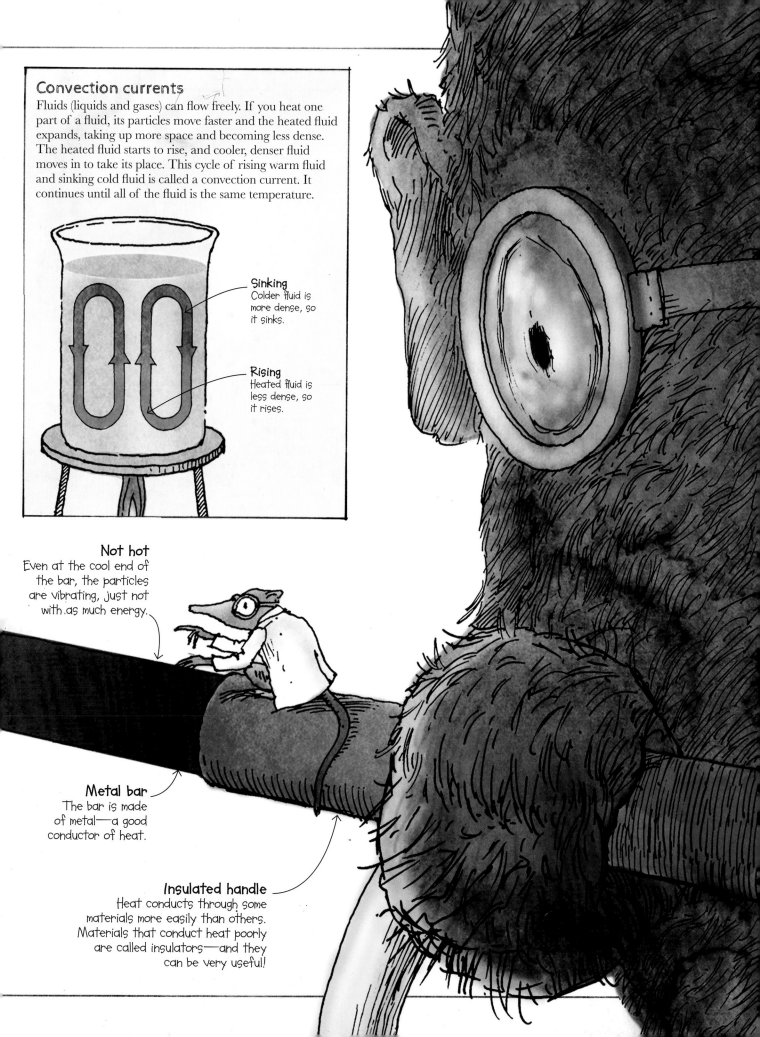

Convection currents

Fluids (liquids and gases) can flow freely. If you heat one part of a fluid, its particles move faster and the heated fluid expands, taking up more space and becoming less dense. The heated fluid starts to rise, and cooler, denser fluid moves in to take its place. This cycle of rising warm fluid and sinking cold fluid is called a convection current. It continues until all of the fluid is the same temperature.

Sinking
Colder fluid is more dense, so it sinks.

Rising
Heated fluid is less dense, so it rises.

Not hot
Even at the cool end of the bar, the particles are vibrating, just not with as much energy.

Metal bar
The bar is made of metal—a good conductor of heat.

Insulated handle
Heat conducts through some materials more easily than others. Materials that conduct heat poorly are called insulators—and they can be very useful!

Sound waves

From a whisper to a bang, all sounds are made by objects that vibrate rapidly to and fro. When you pluck a guitar string, the string vibrates and disturbs the air around it, squashing and stretching the air many times a second. In turn, the squashed and stretched air disturbs the air next to it, so that the disturbance travels as invisible waves spreading out in all directions like ripples on a pond.

Mammoth music

This mammoth maestro is forcing air out through its trunk, and the escaping air is making the skin of the trunk vibrate. This disturbs the air around it, sending a wave of sound through the air. The large waves have lots of energy and make a big sound—loud enough to knock the socks off anyone in the way!

Trumpeting trunk
The mammoth's vibrating trunk produces a low-pitched, booming sound.

Air around the vibrating trunk is disturbed

Squeaky sound
The elephant shrew's quieter, high-pitched squeak is made from smaller waves that are closer together.

Seeing sound waves

Sound waves are usually represented by wavy lines. The shape of the line tells you what the sound is like—whether it is loud or quiet, a high-pitched squeak or a low-pitched boom.

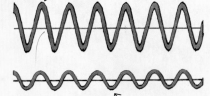

Low-pitched sound
A greater wavelength (distance between each peak) means a lower frequency and a lower pitch.

Loud sound
The taller the peaks and lower the troughs of a sound wave, the louder the sound.

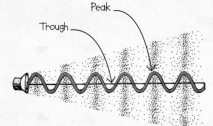

Peak

Trough

Quieter sound

Sound wave
When we draw a sound wave, the peak of the wave shows where the air is compressed. The lowest point, or trough, is where the air is more spread out.

Pitch
The pitch of a sound depends on the wavelength and frequency (how many peaks pass by each second). A high-pitched sound has a short wavelength and a high frequency.

Loudness
The height of a sound wave is called its amplitude. A higher amplitude means a louder sound. These two waves have the same frequency but different amplitudes.

More compressed
The air particles here are squashed together. This is the peak of the sound wave.

Less compressed
The air particles here are more spread out. This is the trough of the wave.

Letting light through

Most solid objects are opaque—they block all light—but some materials allow light waves to pass through. Translucent materials let some light through, but scatter it in all directions. Transparent materials allow light to pass straight through.

Opaque
The elephant shrew is not visible behind a white note card. All the light is blocked.

Translucent
Behind a sheet of tracing paper, the elephant shrew is visible but blurry.

Transparent
A sheet of glass allows virtually all light to pass through. The elephant shrew is clearly visible.

Light

This super-size shadow may look like a woolly mammoth, but it is just a trick of the light. Light is a form of energy that we can see. It only travels in straight lines, or rays, so solid objects cast shadows where they block light's path. Light bouncing off objects is what makes them visible to our eyes.

Strike a pose
Three elephant shrews have blocked some of the light from the torch.

Shadow play

A group of elephant shrews are playing shadow puppets, casting a mammoth silhouette on the wall behind. Shadows are dark, but not completely black because some light can still reach them, reflected off other objects.

Bright beam
Light sources, such as this flashlight, produce their own light.

Big and blurry
The shadow is much larger than the shrews themselves. This is because they are close to the light source and further from the wall, and the light rays spread out as they travel.

Small and sharp
The elephant shrew further from the light source casts a smaller, sharper shadow.

In the spotlight
Objects in the beam of light are visible because light bounces off them and into your eyes.

Reflection

Most things reflect light—we see an object when light bounces off it and enters our eyes. The smooth, shiny surface of a mirror reflects light in a particular way that creates a reflection, or mirror image. This mystified mammoth has encountered some odd reflections in a hall of mirrors.

Misshapen mammoths

Three mirrors are showing three big, bulky reflections—but why are two of the reflections so distorted? In the flat mirror, the mammoth's reflection is a perfect mirror image because all of the light rays are reflected in the same direction. But the mirrors to the left and right are curved, stretching and squashing the mammoth's reflection.

Concave
Where the mirror curves inward, the mammoth looks stretched.

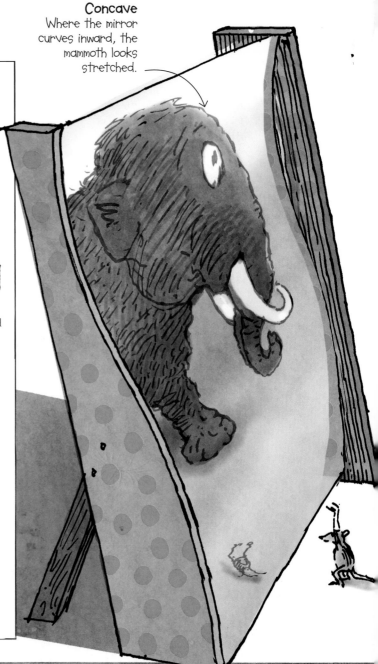

How mirrors work

Mirrors, metals, and other shiny surfaces create reflections because light bounces off them in a very regular way. This is known as specular reflection. When light bounces off a rough surface, it is scattered in different directions. This is called diffuse reflection.

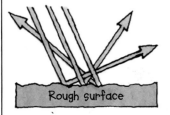 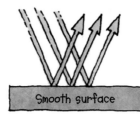

Rough surface   Smooth surface

Bouncing off
When light rays hit a rough surface, such as paper, they are reflected in many directions. Shine light onto a flat, shiny surface, such as a mirror, and the light rays are all reflected in the same direction.

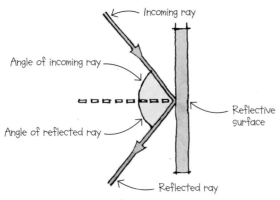

Incoming ray

Angle of incoming ray

Angle of reflected ray

Reflective surface

Reflected ray

Law of reflection
Mirrors reflect light in such a regular way because light rays always bounce off them at the same angle at which they arrived. This is called the law of reflection.

Mirror image

When you look into a mirror, you will see a mirror image of yourself. But the image appears to be standing behind the mirror. This is because the light rays entering your eyes appear to come from behind the mirror. The image of an object in a mirror is called a virtual image, and it is always the same distance behind the mirror as the object is in front of it.

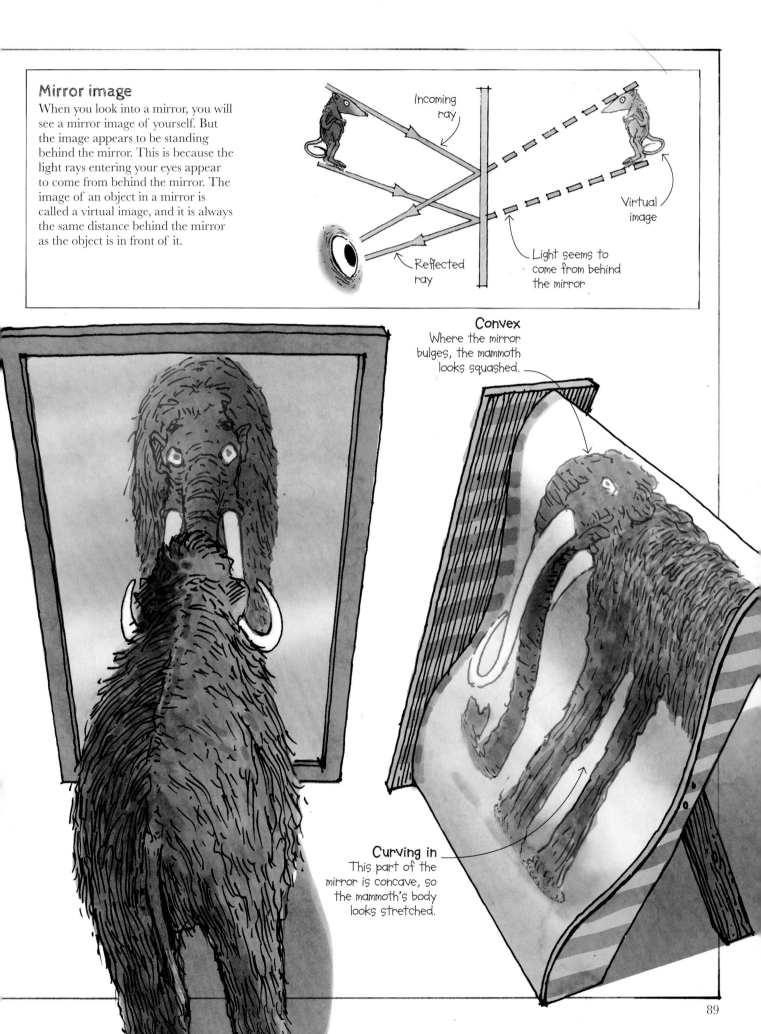

Incoming ray

Virtual image

Reflected ray

Light seems to come from behind the mirror

Convex
Where the mirror bulges, the mammoth looks squashed.

Curving in
This part of the mirror is concave, so the mammoth's body looks stretched.

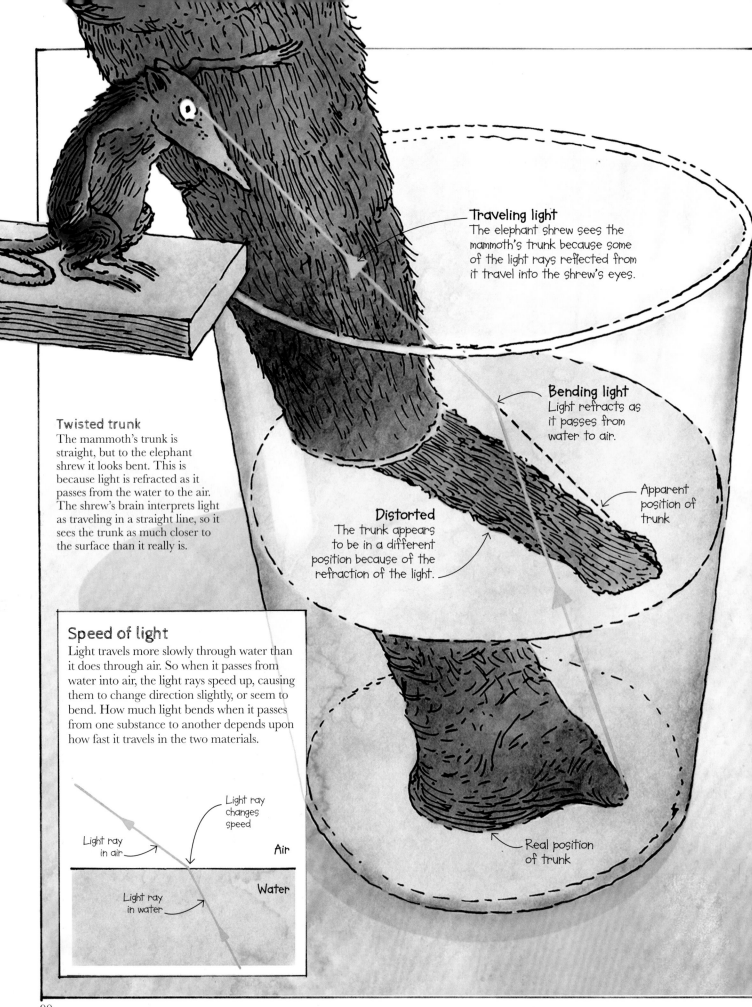

Traveling light
The elephant shrew sees the mammoth's trunk because some of the light rays reflected from it travel into the shrew's eyes.

Bending light
Light refracts as it passes from water to air.

Apparent position of trunk

Distorted
The trunk appears to be in a different position because of the refraction of the light.

Twisted trunk
The mammoth's trunk is straight, but to the elephant shrew it looks bent. This is because light is refracted as it passes from the water to the air. The shrew's brain interprets light as traveling in a straight line, so it sees the trunk as much closer to the surface than it really is.

Real position of trunk

Speed of light
Light travels more slowly through water than it does through air. So when it passes from water into air, the light rays speed up, causing them to change direction slightly, or seem to bend. How much light bends when it passes from one substance to another depends upon how fast it travels in the two materials.

Light ray changes speed

Light ray in air

Air

Water

Light ray in water

Refraction

Light normally travels in straight lines, but it can sometimes bend, or refract. Refraction happens because rays of light travel at different speeds through different substances. They pass quickly through air but slow down when they move through water or glass. Refraction can play tricks, distorting our view, but it can also be useful.

Tricks of the light

When light is refracted, it can trick our brains into seeing things in the wrong place. If you put a pencil in a glass of water, it will look crooked even though it's not. Lenses are specially shaped pieces of glass or transparent plastic that put these tricks of the light to good use.

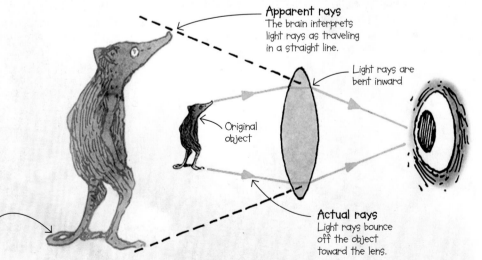

Magnifying glass
A magnifying glass has a convex lens—one that bulges in the middle.

Colossal critter
The elephant shrew standing behind the magnifying glass looks supersized because of the way the light is refracted as it passes through the lens.

Convex lens

When light rays from an object travel through a convex lens, they bend inward and converge (come together) on the other side of the lens. This makes the light rays appear to have come from a much larger object, making the object look bigger than it really is.

Apparent rays
The brain interprets light rays as traveling in a straight line.

Light rays are bent inward

Original object

Virtual image
The image seen through the lens is called a virtual image.

Actual rays
Light rays bounce off the object toward the lens.

White light

The sunlight sneaking in through this doorway may look white, but it's actually a combination of many different colors of light mixed together. When white light travels through a glass prism, the colors separate into a rainbow pattern, called the visible spectrum. There is an infinite number of colors in the spectrum, but our eyes are able to identify seven: red, orange, yellow, green, blue, indigo, and violet.

Making a rainbow

When white light passes through a glass prism, the light refracts (bends; see page 90) as it passes from air to glass and then back to air again. Each color of light bends by a different amount, so the colors all spread out. Raindrops can also act like prisms—that's how rainbows are made.

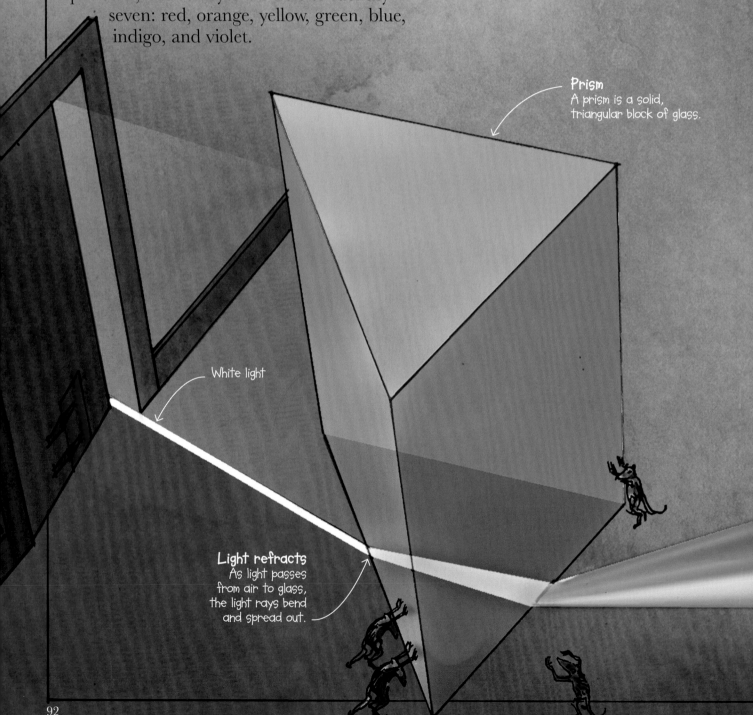

Prism
A prism is a solid, triangular block of glass.

White light

Light refracts
As light passes from air to glass, the light rays bend and spread out.

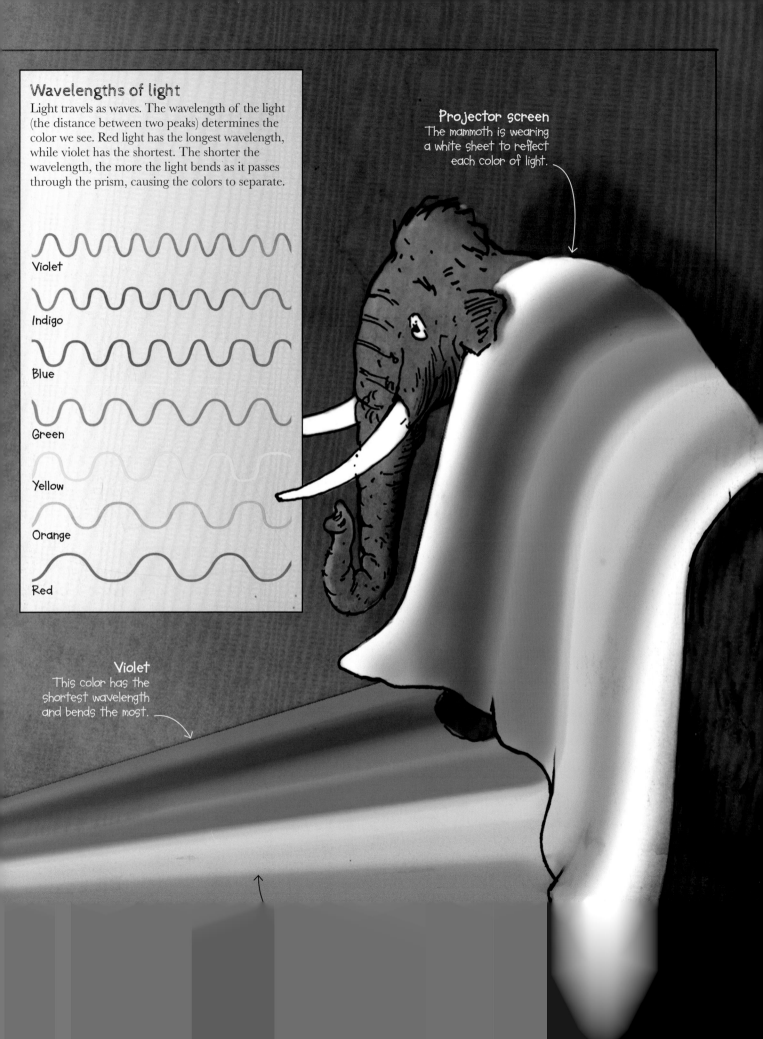

Wavelengths of light

Light travels as waves. The wavelength of the light (the distance between two peaks) determines the color we see. Red light has the longest wavelength, while violet has the shortest. The shorter the wavelength, the more the light bends as it passes through the prism, causing the colors to separate.

Violet

Indigo

Blue

Green

Yellow

Orange

Red

Projector screen
The mammoth is wearing a white sheet to reflect each color of light.

Violet
This color has the shortest wavelength and bends the most.

Seeing color

Our world is bursting with color. From the rich brown of a mammoth's fur to the glossy green of a watermelon, objects only look colorful because of the way they reflect the light. Pigments in their surface absorb light of some colors and reflect others.

Sunlight
Sunlight looks white but is actually made up of all the colors of the rainbow.

Green light
Only green light is reflected into the mammoth's eyes, so the watermelon looks green.

Mouthwatering melon
The mammoth can see the melon because light bounces off it, and some of that light enters the mammoth's eyes. The light hitting the melon is a mixture of all the colors of the rainbow. But pigments in the melon's skin absorb light of all the colors except for green—so only the green light is reflected.

Absorbed
Pigments in the melon's skin absorb all the colors except green.

Mixing colors
Some pigments reflect a mixture of different colors. Pink objects reflect lots of red light and a little bit of all the other colors.

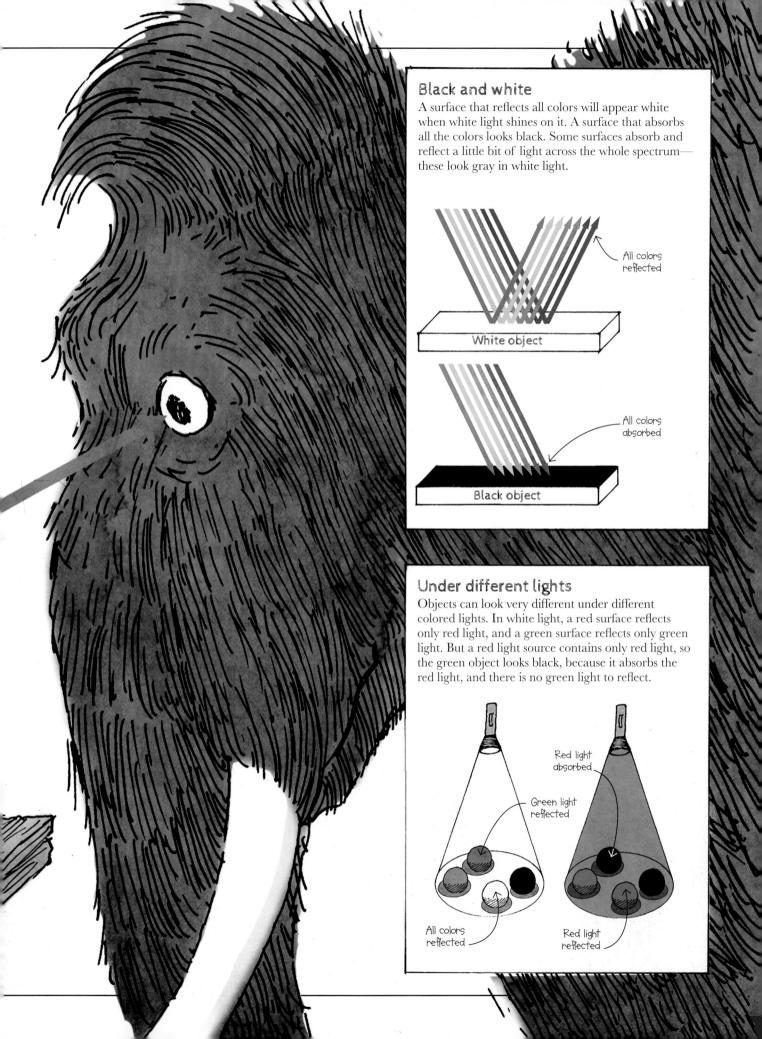

Black and white

A surface that reflects all colors will appear white when white light shines on it. A surface that absorbs all the colors looks black. Some surfaces absorb and reflect a little bit of light across the whole spectrum—these look gray in white light.

All colors reflected

White object

All colors absorbed

Black object

Under different lights

Objects can look very different under different colored lights. In white light, a red surface reflects only red light, and a green surface reflects only green light. But a red light source contains only red light, so the green object looks black, because it absorbs the red light, and there is no green light to reflect.

Red light absorbed

Green light reflected

All colors reflected

Red light reflected

Electromagnetic radiation

The light that we see around us is a type of energy-carrying wave called electromagnetic radiation. Each color of light has a different wavelength—red has the longest and violet the shortest. There are other types of electromagnetic radiation that we cannot see, which have wavelengths shorter or longer than those of visible light.

Infrared image

Infrared is a type of electromagnetic radiation with wavelengths longer than visible light. All objects produce infrared: our eyes cannot see it, but we feel it as heat. This thermal imaging camera detects heat and shows the infrared wavelengths on screen as different colors. The warm-blooded mammoth shows up bright red, while the cold ice cream looks black.

Electromagnetic spectrum

Together, the different types of electromagnetic wave form the electromagnetic spectrum. All travel at the speed of light, but they have different wavelengths (the distance between two peaks), giving them different properties. The shorter the wavelength, the more energy the wave transfers.

Hot body, cold snack
The mammoth's body gives off lots of infrared; the chilly ice cream emits very little.

Low energy
Waves with longer wavelengths transfer less energy.

Radio waves
The longest electromagnetic waves are radio waves, and they transfer the least energy. Radio and television signals use radio waves, as do satellite navigation systems.

Microwaves
The very shortest radio waves are called microwaves. Inside a microwave oven, powerful microwaves cause the food's molecules to jiggle around faster, heating up the food and cooking it.

Infrared
The atoms of all objects are constantly vibrating—this movement generates infrared radiation. The hotter the object the faster the particles vibrate, and the more infrared radiation is emitted.

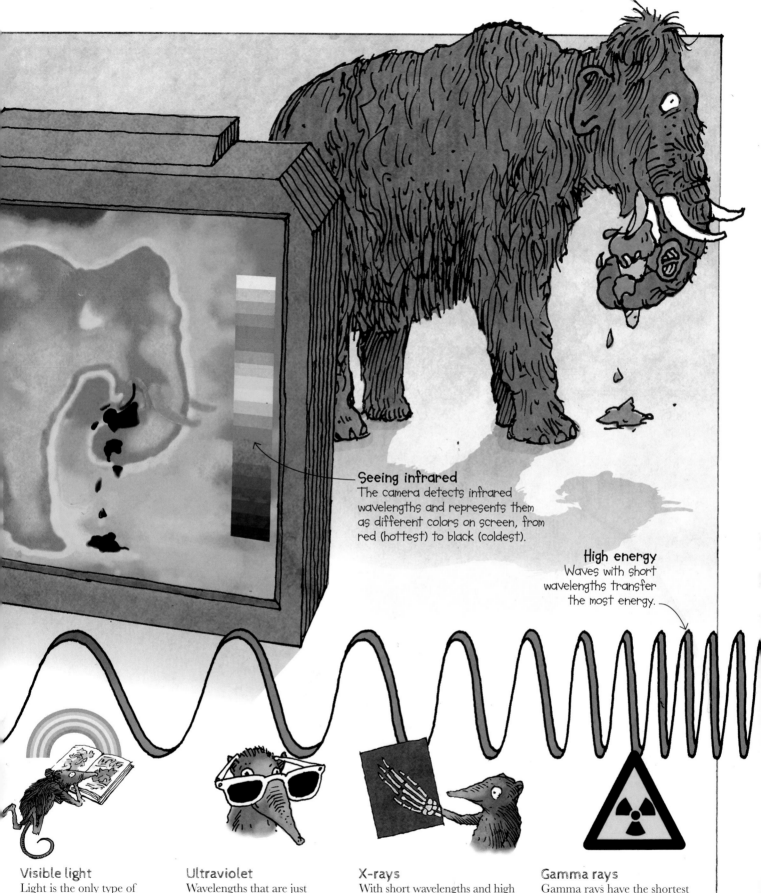

Seeing infrared
The camera detects infrared wavelengths and represents them as different colors on screen, from red (hottest) to black (coldest).

High energy
Waves with short wavelengths transfer the most energy.

Visible light
Light is the only type of electromagnetic wave we can see. Red light has the longest wavelength and violet light has the shortest.

Ultraviolet
Wavelengths that are just shorter than visible violet light are called ultraviolet (UV). UV rays from the sun can damage our eyes and skin.

X-rays
With short wavelengths and high energy, these waves are used to view inside our bodies. They travel through soft tissues but are absorbed by bones.

Gamma rays
Gamma rays have the shortest wavelength and transfer the most energy. They come from radioactive materials and massive stars exploding in space.

Static electricity

The tiny, negatively charged particles inside atoms are called electrons. Electrons can move around and even transfer from one object to another. When electrons build up in one place, objects can gain a "static" electric charge.

Fairground fun

The elephant shrews are using science to set up their fairground attraction. Rubbing a balloon against the mammoth's bristly hair transfers electrons from the hair to the balloon. This creates a negative charge that allows the balloon to stick to a wall as if by magic. Perfect for a game of balloon darts!

Opposites attract

Positive and negative charges attract each other, but like charges repel (push each other away). The negative charge on a charged balloon pushes away the negative charges inside the wall, leaving the wall's surface with a positive charge. The positive and negative charges attract, making the balloon cling to the wall.

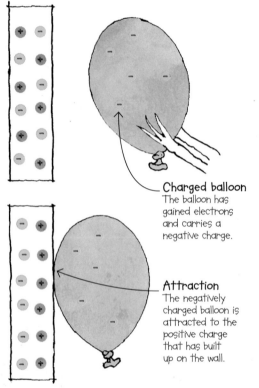

Charged balloon
The balloon has gained electrons and carries a negative charge.

Attraction
The negatively charged balloon is attracted to the positive charge that has built up on the wall.

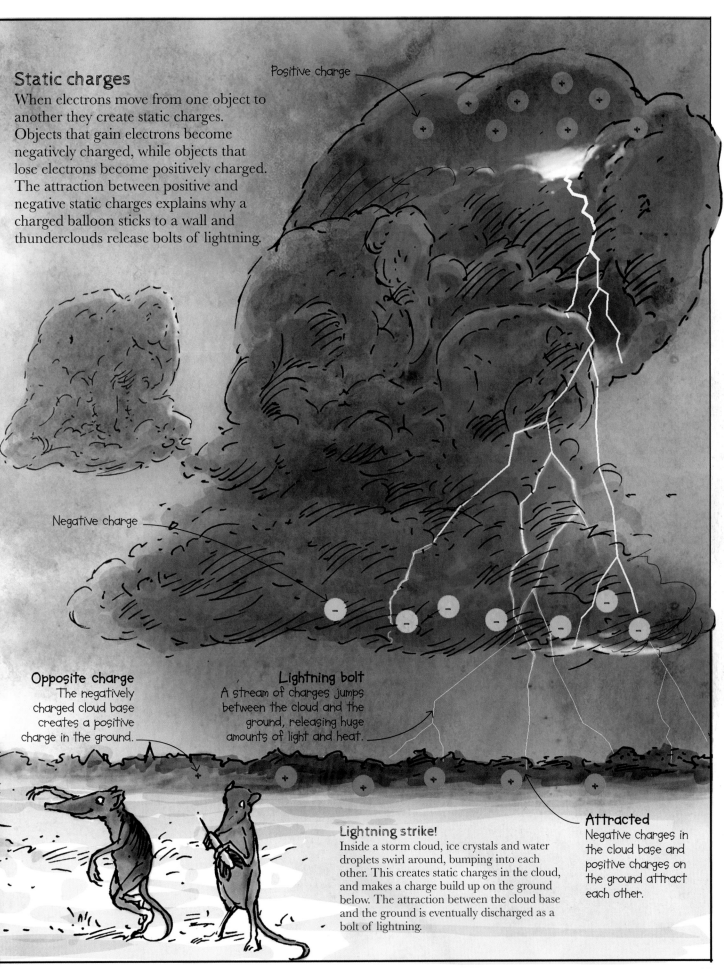

Static charges

When electrons move from one object to another they create static charges. Objects that gain electrons become negatively charged, while objects that lose electrons become positively charged. The attraction between positive and negative static charges explains why a charged balloon sticks to a wall and thunderclouds release bolts of lightning.

Positive charge

Negative charge

Opposite charge
The negatively charged cloud base creates a positive charge in the ground.

Lightning bolt
A stream of charges jumps between the cloud and the ground, releasing huge amounts of light and heat.

Attracted
Negative charges in the cloud base and positive charges on the ground attract each other.

Lightning strike!
Inside a storm cloud, ice crystals and water droplets swirl around, bumping into each other. This creates static charges in the cloud, and makes a charge build up on the ground below. The attraction between the cloud base and the ground is eventually discharged as a bolt of lightning.

Wire loop game

The aim of this electrifying game is to move the wire loop all the way around the wire mammoth without letting the two wires touch. When the wires aren't touching, the circuit is not complete and current can't flow. But it needs a steady hand—as soon as this elephant shrew slips up and makes contact, the current flows and the bulb lights up.

Conductor
Metals like this copper wire are conductors— electric current can flow through them.

Making contact
When the loop touches the wire, the circuit is completed and the light bulb comes on.

Insulator
Most materials, such as the plastic coating on this wire, do not conduct electricity.

Power supply
The battery provides the energy that pushes the electrons around the circuit.

Electric current

Electricity powers our lives—from light bulbs to cell phones, and household appliances to electric vehicles. The electric current that runs through all these devices is a flow of negatively charged particles called electrons. A current can only flow when there is a complete, unbroken path or circuit for it to move around, and a power supply such as a battery to get the electrons moving.

No current
This part of the wire—beyond where the loop touches the mammoth—is not part of the circuit and no current flows through it.

Light bulb on
The moving electrons transfer energy stored in the battery to the bulb, making it light up.

Inside the wire

In a metal wire, some electrons are free to move around. If the wire is connected to a battery in a complete, unbroken circuit, these electrons will all move in the same direction—from the negative side of a battery to the positive side. This flow of electrons is called electric current.

No current
The electrons move around randomly in all directions.

Flowing current
When the wire is part of a circuit, the electrons all move in the same direction.

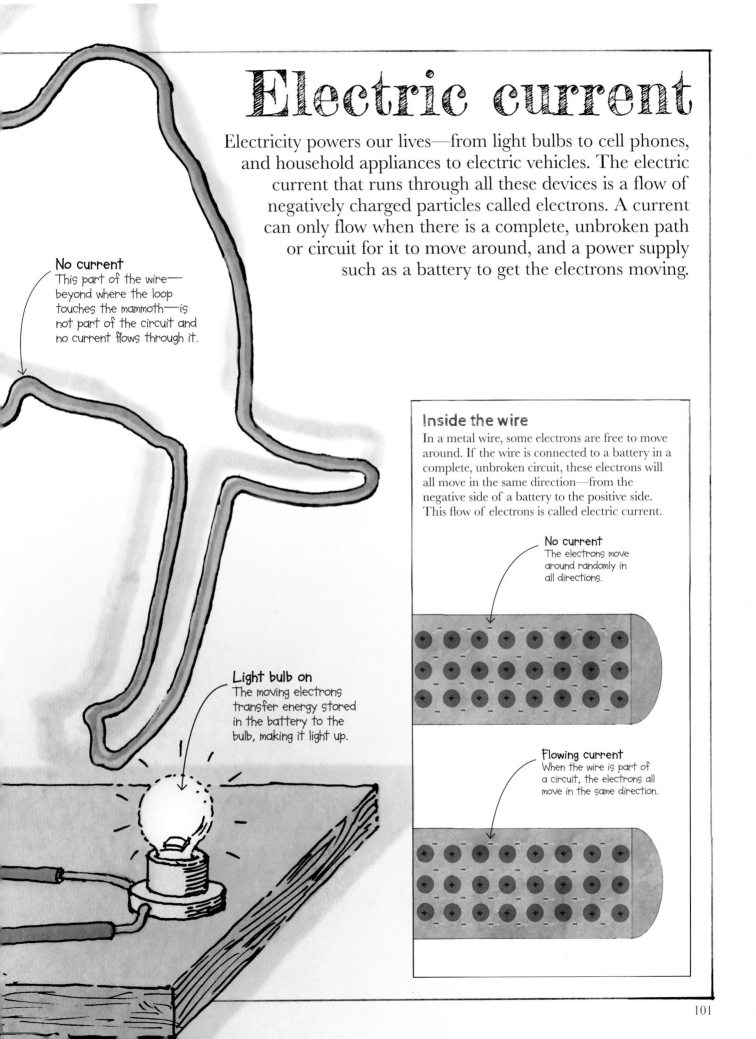

Magnetism

These mighty mammoths are straining hard, but they can't overcome the force between two giant horseshoe magnets. Magnetism is an invisible force that can pull together or push apart objects without actually touching them.

Forces in action

Horseshoe magnets are curved into a U-shape, but like all magnets they have two ends, or "poles." The north pole is usually shown in red and the south pole in blue. Magnets will attract and repel other magnets depending on how the two poles line up.

Opposites attract
The opposite poles of the magnets are lined up so the magnets stick together.

North pole

South pole

Magnetic materials

Materials that are attracted to magnets are called magnetic materials. These include metals such as iron, nickel, cobalt, and steel. When they are placed inside a magnetic field, these materials are temporarily magnetized themselves, gaining a north and south pole.

Iron nails
These iron nails turn into miniature magnets when they are near the horseshoe magnet.

Invisible barrier

This pair of pachyderms are trying to push the magnets together. But now the poles are lined up north to north and south to south, so the magnets repel each other. The invisible magnetic force means that the magnets won't touch.

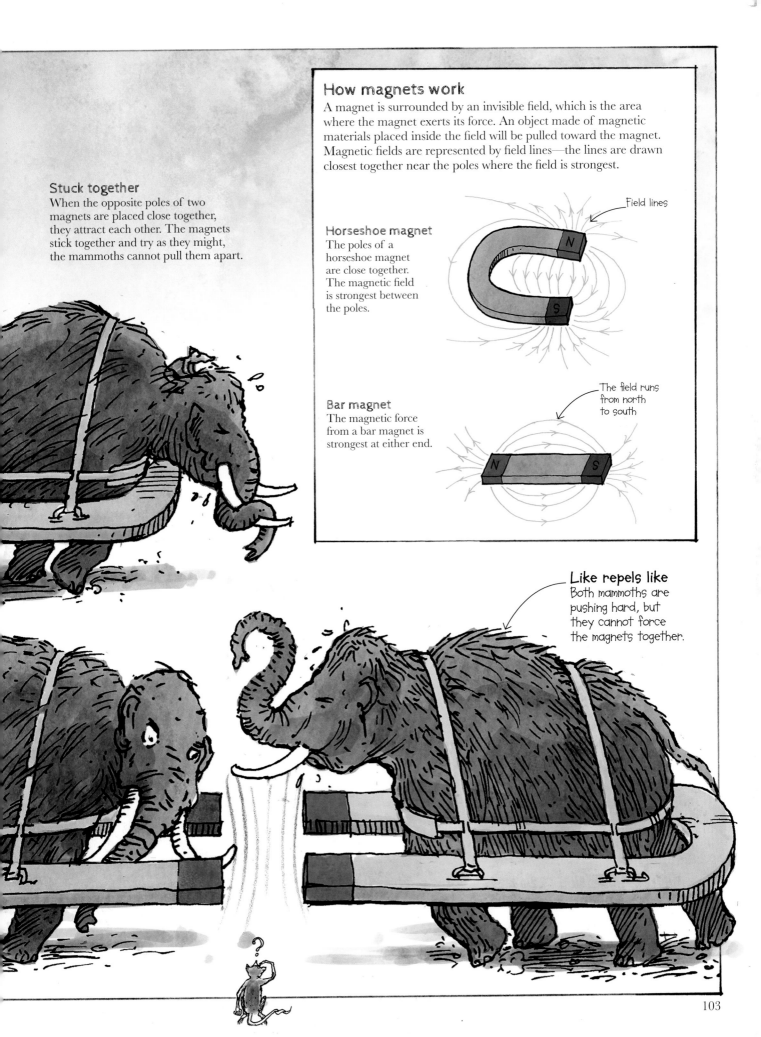

Stuck together

When the opposite poles of two magnets are placed close together, they attract each other. The magnets stick together and try as they might, the mammoths cannot pull them apart.

How magnets work

A magnet is surrounded by an invisible field, which is the area where the magnet exerts its force. An object made of magnetic materials placed inside the field will be pulled toward the magnet. Magnetic fields are represented by field lines—the lines are drawn closest together near the poles where the field is strongest.

Field lines

Horseshoe magnet

The poles of a horseshoe magnet are close together. The magnetic field is strongest between the poles.

N

S

The field runs from north to south

Bar magnet

The magnetic force from a bar magnet is strongest at either end.

N   S

Like repels like

Both mammoths are pushing hard, but they cannot force the magnets together.

Forces

Tug of war

When two or more forces are at work, they combine to act as a single force. If the forces are equal and acting in opposite directions, they balance each other and nothing happens. The mammoths taking part in this tug of war are both pulling hard, but the overall force is zero, until some teammates pitch in.

Deadlock

Two mammoths are pulling with equal force in opposite directions. The forces cancel each other out, so neither mammoth moves.

Balanced forces

Both mammoths are pulling with a force of 1,000 N, so the overall force is 0 N.

What are forces?

A force is a push or a pull. You can't see a force but you can see what it does: forces can change the speed or direction of a moving object, or slow it down to a stop. They can also squash or stretch an object so that it changes shape. The mammoths here are using their muscles to try to exert a force that will pull the other one over.

1,000 newtons

1,000 newtons

1,000 newtons

1,020 newtons

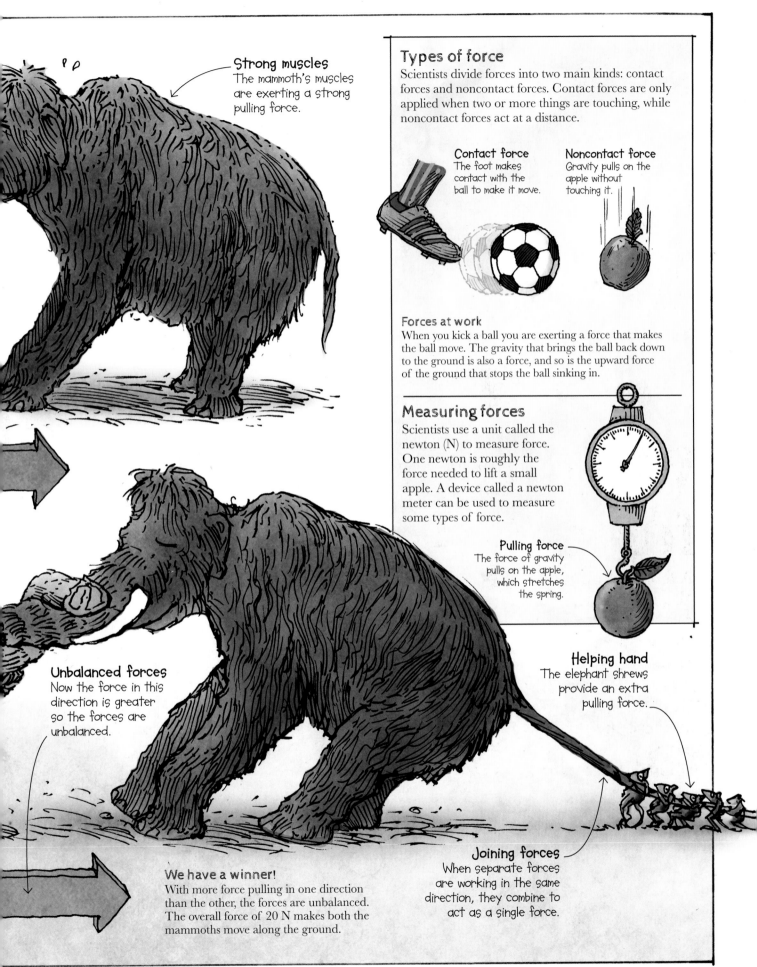

Strong muscles
The mammoth's muscles are exerting a strong pulling force.

Types of force
Scientists divide forces into two main kinds: contact forces and noncontact forces. Contact forces are only applied when two or more things are touching, while noncontact forces act at a distance.

Contact force
The foot makes contact with the ball to make it move.

Noncontact force
Gravity pulls on the apple without touching it.

Forces at work
When you kick a ball you are exerting a force that makes the ball move. The gravity that brings the ball back down to the ground is also a force, and so is the upward force of the ground that stops the ball sinking in.

Measuring forces
Scientists use a unit called the newton (N) to measure force. One newton is roughly the force needed to lift a small apple. A device called a newton meter can be used to measure some types of force.

Pulling force
The force of gravity pulls on the apple, which stretches the spring.

Unbalanced forces
Now the force in this direction is greater so the forces are unbalanced.

Helping hand
The elephant shrews provide an extra pulling force.

We have a winner!
With more force pulling in one direction than the other, the forces are unbalanced. The overall force of 20 N makes both the mammoths move along the ground.

Joining forces
When separate forces are working in the same direction, they combine to act as a single force.

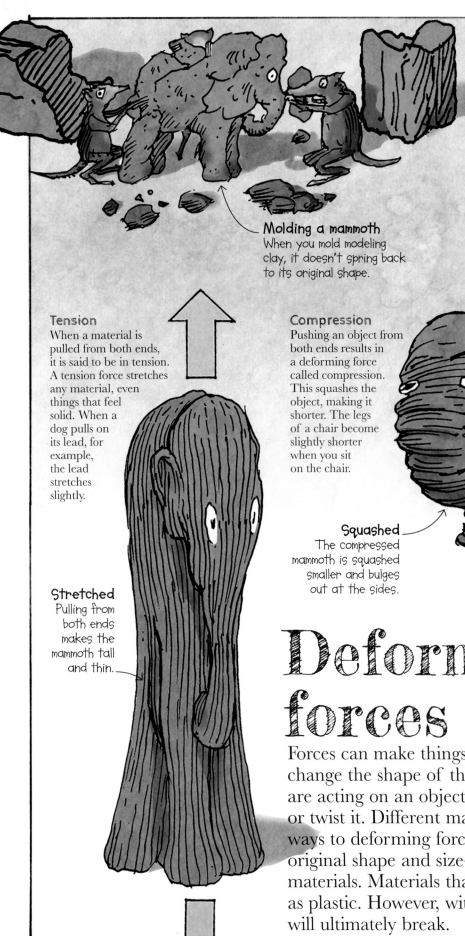

Mashed-up mammoths

In order to make a mammoth from modeling clay, these elephant shrews need to use deforming forces, to get just the right shape. They squeeze and stretch the clay, and twist and bend it, to make the perfect mammoth model. Once the model has been made, applying those same deforming forces can change its shape in crazy ways.

Molding a mammoth
When you mold modeling clay, it doesn't spring back to its original shape.

Tension
When a material is pulled from both ends, it is said to be in tension. A tension force stretches any material, even things that feel solid. When a dog pulls on its lead, for example, the lead stretches slightly.

Compression
Pushing an object from both ends results in a deforming force called compression. This squashes the object, making it shorter. The legs of a chair become slightly shorter when you sit on the chair.

Squashed
The compressed mammoth is squashed smaller and bulges out at the sides.

Stretched
Pulling from both ends makes the mammoth tall and thin.

Deforming forces

Forces can make things move, but they can also change the shape of things. When two or more forces are acting on an object, they can stretch, squash, bend, or twist it. Different materials respond in different ways to deforming forces. Some will return to their original shape and size—these are called elastic materials. Materials that stay deformed are described as plastic. However, with enough force all materials will ultimately break.

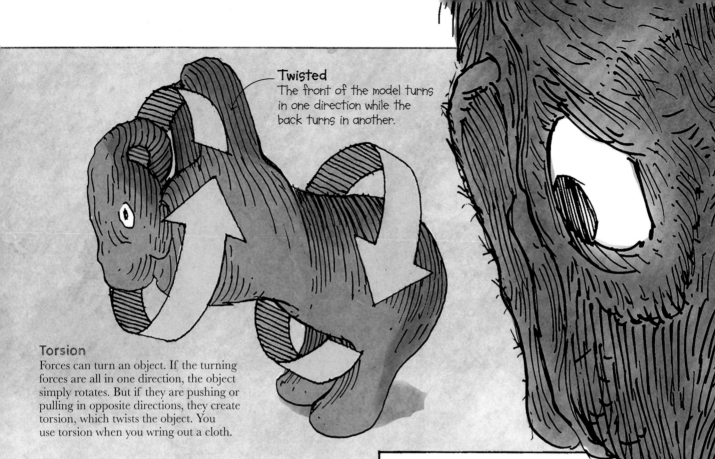

Twisted
The front of the model turns in one direction while the back turns in another.

Torsion

Forces can turn an object. If the turning forces are all in one direction, the object simply rotates. But if they are pushing or pulling in opposite directions, they create torsion, which twists the object. You use torsion when you wring out a cloth.

Bending

Two or more forces applied in different places and in different directions can make an object bend. Even things we don't think of as bendy will bend slightly—such as a tall building on a windy day or a bridge when you stand on it.

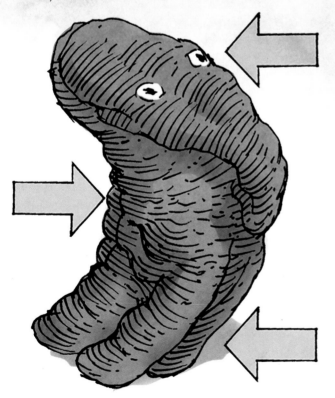

How materials deform

Modeling clay is a plastic material: it retains its new shape even after the deforming forces no longer act. Many materials are elastic, returning to their original size and shape. Metals are elastic up to a certain point—but if you pull them very hard or squash them strongly, they will permanently deform, and eventually they will break.

Elasticity

A metal spring will stretch if a force is applied, and then return to its original unstretched shape after the force is removed. But if you apply too much force and stretch it too much, it will remain permanently stretched. The point of no return is called a material's elastic limit.

Brittle materials

Most materials will eventually break if you apply enough force. Some brittle materials, such as glass and ceramics, will reach breaking point with almost no deformation first. If you drop a ceramic cup on a hard surface it will crack or shatter.

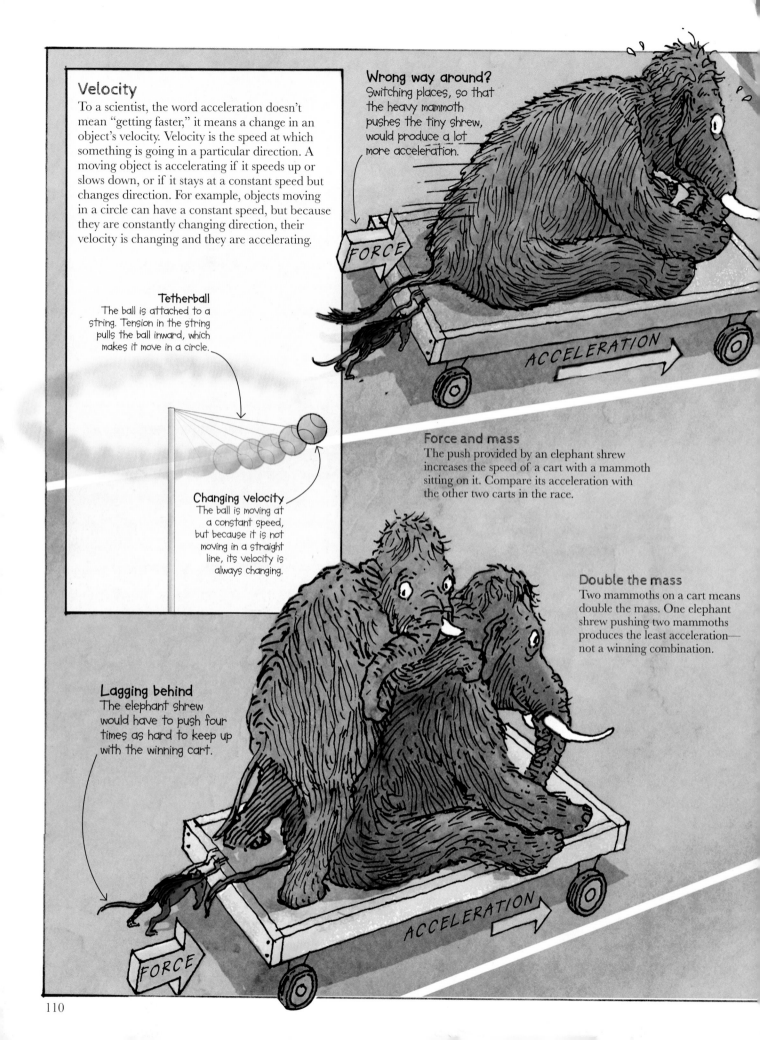

Velocity

To a scientist, the word acceleration doesn't mean "getting faster," it means a change in an object's velocity. Velocity is the speed at which something is going in a particular direction. A moving object is accelerating if it speeds up or slows down, or if it stays at a constant speed but changes direction. For example, objects moving in a circle can have a constant speed, but because they are constantly changing direction, their velocity is changing and they are accelerating.

Tetherball
The ball is attached to a string. Tension in the string pulls the ball inward, which makes it move in a circle.

Changing velocity
The ball is moving at a constant speed, but because it is not moving in a straight line, its velocity is always changing.

Wrong way around?
Switching places, so that the heavy mammoth pushes the tiny shrew, would produce a lot more acceleration.

FORCE

ACCELERATION

Force and mass
The push provided by an elephant shrew increases the speed of a cart with a mammoth sitting on it. Compare its acceleration with the other two carts in the race.

Double the mass
Two mammoths on a cart means double the mass. One elephant shrew pushing two mammoths produces the least acceleration—not a winning combination.

Lagging behind
The elephant shrew would have to push four times as hard to keep up with the winning cart.

FORCE

ACCELERATION

Acceleration

If you want to make something go faster, you need to push it or pull it. How quickly the object's speed changes—its acceleration—depends on the size of the force. In this race, mammoth-carrying carts are being pushed along by energetic elephant shrews. The carts accelerate as long as the shrews keep pushing. The cart with the greatest acceleration will reach the highest speed and win the race. But look carefully—it's not a level playing field.

Upping the odds
If the mammoth were to lose weight, it would accelerate even faster next time.

Mammoth movers

There was only ever going to be one winner in this mammoth-cart race. This is because an object's acceleration depends not just on the force applied, but also on the object's mass. If you use the same force to push two objects of different masses, the lighter one will accelerate more quickly. But if both objects have the same mass, then more force means more acceleration.

Double the force
Two elephant shrews pushing a single mammoth produce the most acceleration, so this cart easily wins the race.

Over the line
Two elephant shrews push with double the force of just one.

FORCE

FORCE

ACCELERATION

Go, go, go!
The mammoth at the back crashes into its neighbor.

Momentum

A speeding train, a rolling ball, a swinging mammoth—some moving objects can be hard to stop. This is because they have lots of momentum. The more mass an object has and the faster it is going, the more momentum it has. When a moving object collides with something, its momentum can be transferred—as demonstrated by this troupe of plucky stunt mammoths.

Collision course

Five high-flying mammoths are dangling from wires. The mammoth at one end of the row is pulled back, then released. Traveling through the air, it smashes into the row of stationary mammoths. The first mammoth then stops moving, but its momentum is transferred along the line, from one helmeted heavyweight to the next, until the final mammoth is flung forward into the air.

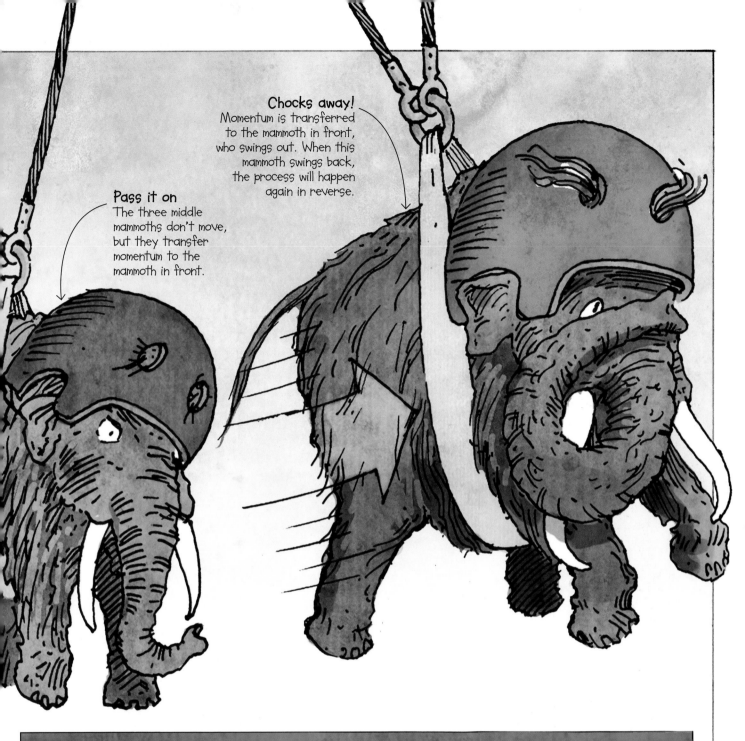

Pass it on
The three middle mammoths don't move, but they transfer momentum to the mammoth in front.

Chocks away!
Momentum is transferred to the mammoth in front, who swings out. When this mammoth swings back, the process will happen again in reverse.

Conservation of momentum

When objects collide, some may slow down or stop, but the total momentum is the same before and after the collision. This is called the conservation of momentum. In a billiards game, the white cue ball strikes the red balls, which all start moving. Individually, each ball has less momentum than the cue ball did before the collision, but added together the momentum remains the same.

Matching momentum
The combined momentum of all the red balls is the same as that of the white ball before the collision.

Colliding cue ball
The white cue ball hits the red balls and sends them flying.

Action and reaction

Every force, everywhere in the universe, is matched with a twin of the same strength that works in the opposite direction. Another way of saying this is that for every action, there is an equal and opposite reaction. The two forces are equal in strength but are working on different objects, in opposite directions.

Rocket reaction

Blasting into the air from a standing start, this sky-bound mammoth is using action-reaction to defy gravity. The rocket engine strapped to the mammoth's back produces an upward force called thrust by sending out high-pressure gas in the opposite direction. The thrust is enough to overcome the pull of gravity that normally keeps the mammoth firmly on the ground.

Action-reaction rocket

The rocket's thrust is an example of an equal and opposite reaction. When the fuel inside the rocket burns, it produces a large amount of hot exhaust gas. The gas expands and pushes against the inside of the rocket engine, and the rocket engine pushes back against the gas. As a result, the gas is pushed downward at high speed, and the rocket itself is pushed up with equal force.

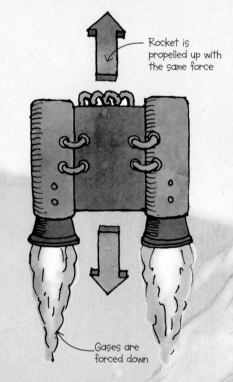

Rocket is propelled up with the same force

Gases are forced down

Earthbound mammoth
This mammoth's weight keeps it firmly on the ground until a force is applied.

... must come down
When the rocket runs out of fuel, the mammoth's weight will bring it back down to Earth.

What goes up ...
The thrust is greater than the mammoth's weight, so the mammoth shoots upward.

WEIGHT

THRUST

On the ground
Even when the mammoth is just standing on the ground, there is an action and reaction taking place. Gravity is pulling the mammoth toward Earth, but it is also pulling Earth toward the mammoth with an equal force.

Gravity pulls Earth toward the mammoth

Gravity pulls the mammoth toward Earth

How gravity works

Gravity is a force that acts between two objects. The pull of gravity is stronger the more mass the objects have and the closer they are together.

Equal force

There is an equal force on each of the two objects, even if they have different masses. The smaller object pulls on the massive object with exactly the same force that the massive one pulls on the smaller one.

Greater mass, more gravity

The size of the force depends on how much mass each object has. Doubling the mass of just one of the objects would double the gravity between them.

Greater distance, less gravity

The pull of gravity weakens the further away the objects are from each other. If the distance doubles, the force is only a quarter of the size.

Gravity

Gravity is the force that keeps the moon in orbit around Earth, and stops us from floating off Earth's surface into space. It acts between any two objects, pulling them toward each other. However, gravity is a weak force, so its effects are only noticeable near objects with enormous masses, such as Earth. The more mass something has the greater the force of gravity.

One giant leap

The moon has much less mass than Earth, so the force of gravity is much weaker there. A mammoth on the moon would be able to jump much higher than on Earth, because the force pulling it back to the surface is not as strong. It really would be one giant leap for mammoth-kind.

Jumping up
The mammoth jumps with enough force to overcome the pull of gravity.

Giant leap
The mammoth's moon jump would be six times higher than on Earth.

Unbalanced forces
The force of gravity between the moon and the mammoth is less than the mammoth's upward force.

Mass and weight

Mass is the amount of matter something has, whereas weight is a force—how much gravity pulls on something. The mammoth's mass is always the same, whether on Earth or the moon, but its weight changes depending on the pull of gravity.

Weight on the moon

On the moon, the mammoth weighs one-sixth of what it does on Earth, because gravity on the moon is one-sixth as strong as it is on Earth. A set of scales shows this different weight, even though the mammoth's mass has not changed.

Weight in deep space

If the mammoth could travel outside the galaxy, far away from any planets or stars, there would be so little gravity that the mammoth would be almost weightless. There would be no force pulling on the mammoth's mass to register on the scales.

Falling down
The mammoth starts to fall back down, pulled by gravity.

Earth
Gravity pulling Earth and the moon together keeps the moon in orbit around Earth.

Moon landing
The mammoth lands back down with a gentle bump.

Friction

If you push or pull an object along a surface there will always be a force that acts in the opposite direction. That force is called friction, and it is created whenever two surfaces rub together. When the mammoth whizzes down a slippery slide, the force of friction is weak, so the mammoth keeps speeding up. But when the mammoth hits the ground, friction increases, and the mammoth is in for a rough ride.

Slippery slide
There isn't much friction between the smooth surface of the slide and the mammoth's furry bottom, so the mammoth shoots down, pulled by gravity.

Stuck bucket
The elephant shrews are struggling to overcome friction between the bucket and the ground.

Everyday friction

Whenever two surfaces move past one another, friction is always at work. Sometimes this is very useful—allowing tires to grip the road or a bicycle's brakes to work, for example. In other situations, friction gets in the way by slowing things down. Friction can also make machines less efficient and wear down their moving parts. Putting a layer of liquid between moving parts reduces friction and stops components wearing down. This is called lubrication.

Get a grip
The soles of shoes are often made of rubber to increase friction and stop us slipping. It is friction that allows us to push ourselves along as we walk.

Reducing friction
The chain and gears of a bicycle can stick. Adding oil makes the surfaces more slippery, allowing them to slide over each other much more smoothly.

Sticking surfaces

To keep an object moving, you have to push or pull with enough force to overcome friction. At the top of the slide, gravity is pulling the mammoth down. But once the mammoth reaches the bottom of the slide, there is no force propelling it forward any more, so when friction increases the mammoth soon slows down.

Rough landing
The mammoth continues to move along the ground. But there is a lot of friction between the mammoth and the rough earth, so the beast soon comes to a halt. If there were slippery ice at the bottom of the slide the mammoth would keep moving longer.

Close-up view
All surfaces have tiny bumps. Friction is created by these bumps rubbing and catching on each other. The rougher the surface, the more bumps and the greater the friction.

Hot bottom
Friction always produces heat, which comes from the energy of the moving object as it slows down.

Turbulence
An irregularly shaped object disturbs the air, creating a swirling motion, called turbulence, which creates more drag.

Hair raising!
Even the mammoth's hair increases drag a tiny bit. As the mammoth moves through the air, each strand provides a bit more surface for the air to push against.

Meeting resistance
With flailing limbs and trunk, and its body held upright, this moving mammoth has lots of surfaces for the air to push against.

Slippery slide
There isn't much friction between the sled and the snowy hillside so the mammoth glides down.

Drag

If you want to move through the air, you have to move the air out of the way. As you push the air, the air pushes back on you, with a force called air resistance, also known as drag. The larger an object is and the faster it is moving, the greater the drag, because the more air there is hitting its surfaces. Air resistance is like friction: it slows down a moving object, just like friction does when solid surfaces rub together.

Drag race

These two mammoths are sliding down the same slope on identical sleds, but one is going faster than the other. The first is sitting upright, providing a big surface for the air to push against, so drag slows this mammoth down. But the other has taken measures to reduce drag, giving this speedy slider the edge in the race.

Flowing air
Air flows easily over the streamlined mammoth, creating less turbulence.

Streamlined shape
By going head first and tucking in limbs and trunk, this mammoth forms a shape that cuts through the air with ease.

Smooth surface
The smooth material of this aerodynamic suit allows air to move over it easily, reducing drag and turbulence.

Drag force

Water resistance is hundreds of times greater than air resistance

Drag force

Water resistance

Just as an object moving through air experiences air resistance, an object moving through water or any other fluid will experience resistance. Water is much more dense than air, so it takes much more force, and more energy, to move the water out of the way. This is why it is much more difficult to push through water than through air, and why boats need a pointed bow (front) and a streamlined shape.

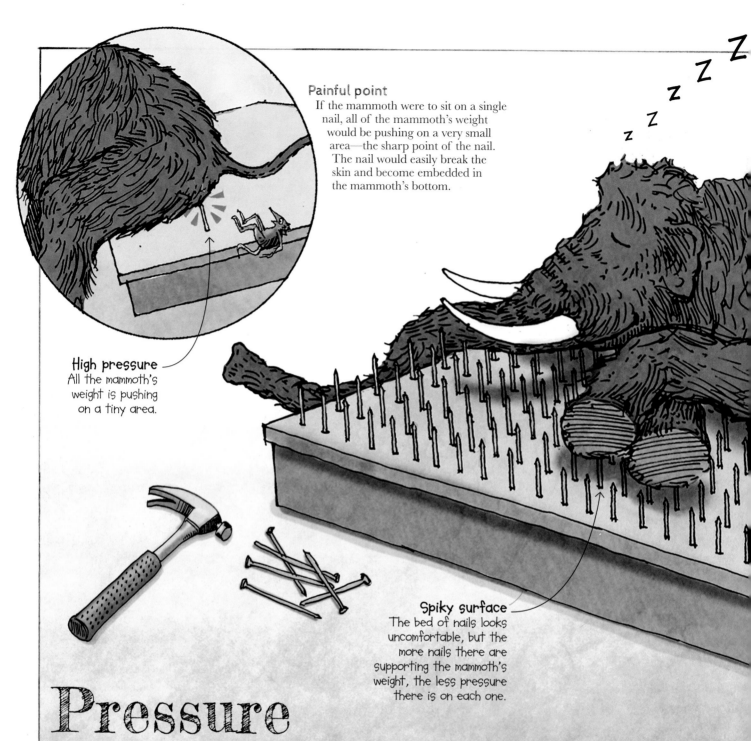

Painful point
If the mammoth were to sit on a single nail, all of the mammoth's weight would be pushing on a very small area—the sharp point of the nail. The nail would easily break the skin and become embedded in the mammoth's bottom.

High pressure
All the mammoth's weight is pushing on a tiny area.

Spiky surface
The bed of nails looks uncomfortable, but the more nails there are supporting the mammoth's weight, the less pressure there is on each one.

Pressure

When a force pushes on something, it exerts pressure. Pressure is the amount that a force is concentrated in one place or spread out. The same force can create high or low pressure depending on how great an area it acts on: the smaller the area, the greater the pressure. For example, thumbtacks and nails are easy to push into surfaces because they have sharp points that concentrate a pushing force in a very small area. The sharper the point, the higher the pressure.

Bed of nails

How come this mammoth looks so comfortable lying on those sharp nails? You'd think the poor pachyderm would end up pierced and punctured, but in fact the way the mammoth's weight is distributed across so many nails means there is only a little bit of pressure on each one. Time for forty winks!

Sleeping easy

On the bed of nails, the mammoth's weight is spread over hundreds of individual nails, so the mammoth is only pressing down on each one a little bit. It really is possible to lie on a bed of nails without getting injured. The tricky bit, especially for mammoths, is getting on and off.

Spreading the load

Now the mammoth's weight is spread across a large number of nails, so the pressure on each one is small.

Fluid pressure

Liquids and gases exert pressure, too. When you blow air into a balloon, for example, the air presses outward, inflating the balloon. Fluids are also squashed by their own weight—and the pressure is stronger the more fluid there is pressing down from above. In a bottle of water, the pressure will be higher at the bottom than at the top. You can show this by making holes in the bottle: water from the bottom will be forced out more quickly than water from the top.

Water only trickles out

Water shoots out at speed

Low pressure

Near the top, there is only a little bit of water above pushing down.

High pressure

At the bottom, the weight of all the water above creates high pressure.

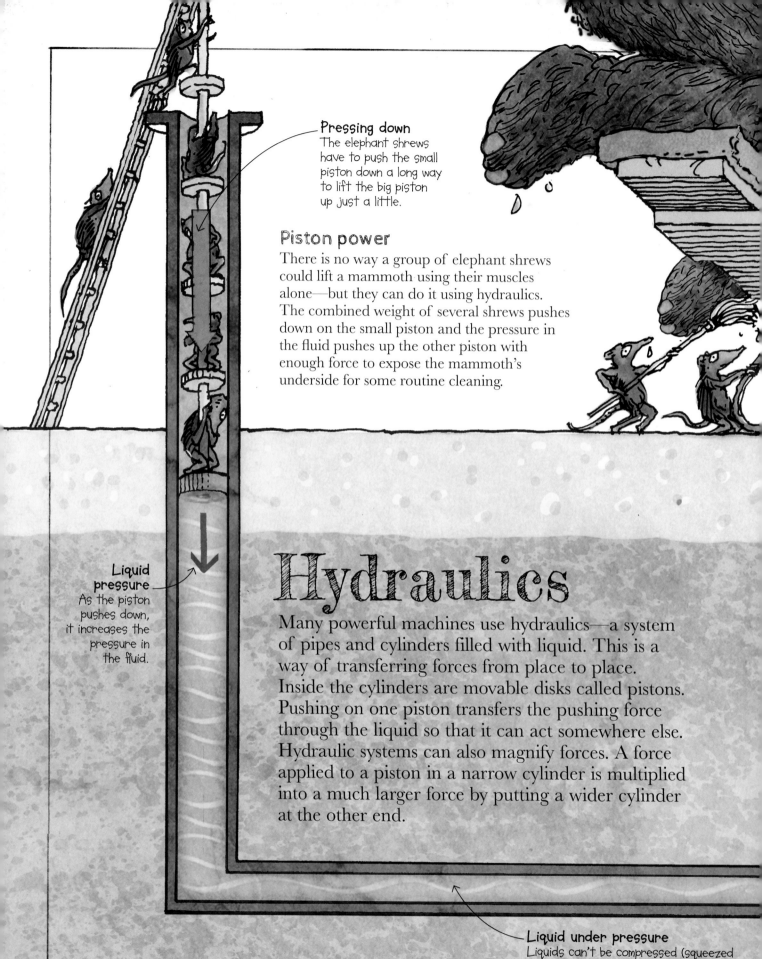

Pressing down
The elephant shrews have to push the small piston down a long way to lift the big piston up just a little.

Piston power

There is no way a group of elephant shrews could lift a mammoth using their muscles alone—but they can do it using hydraulics. The combined weight of several shrews pushes down on the small piston and the pressure in the fluid pushes up the other piston with enough force to expose the mammoth's underside for some routine cleaning.

Liquid pressure
As the piston pushes down, it increases the pressure in the fluid.

Hydraulics

Many powerful machines use hydraulics—a system of pipes and cylinders filled with liquid. This is a way of transferring forces from place to place. Inside the cylinders are movable disks called pistons. Pushing on one piston transfers the pushing force through the liquid so that it can act somewhere else. Hydraulic systems can also magnify forces. A force applied to a piston in a narrow cylinder is multiplied into a much larger force by putting a wider cylinder at the other end.

Liquid under pressure
Liquids can't be compressed (squeezed into a smaller space) so the liquid under pressure pushes out in all directions.

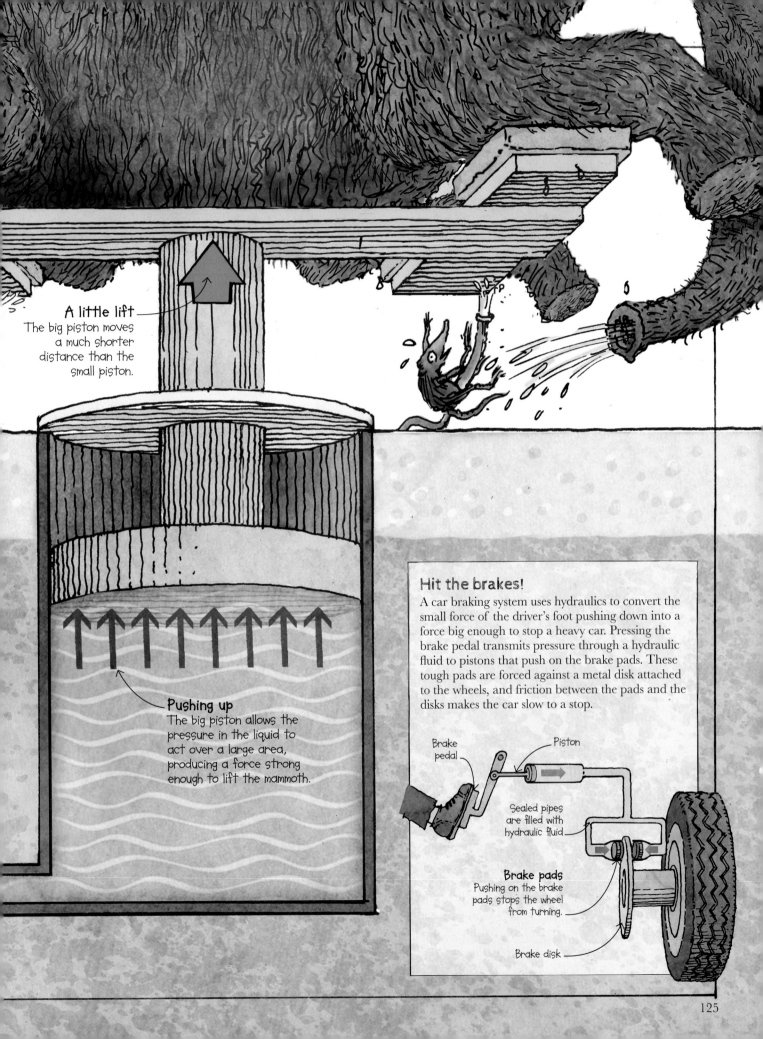

A little lift
The big piston moves a much shorter distance than the small piston.

Pushing up
The big piston allows the pressure in the liquid to act over a large area, producing a force strong enough to lift the mammoth.

Hit the brakes!
A car braking system uses hydraulics to convert the small force of the driver's foot pushing down into a force big enough to stop a heavy car. Pressing the brake pedal transmits pressure through a hydraulic fluid to pistons that push on the brake pads. These tough pads are forced against a metal disk attached to the wheels, and friction between the pads and the disks makes the car slow to a stop.

Brake pedal

Piston

Sealed pipes are filled with hydraulic fluid

Brake pads
Pushing on the brake pads stops the wheel from turning.

Brake disk

Life ring
The mammoth's ring is filled with air, which is much less dense than water.

Up, up, and away!
Objects can float in gases as well as in liquids. This balloon is floating in air because it is filled with helium, a gas that is less dense than air.

Floating
To float with its body above the surface of the water, this mammoth has donned an air-filled ring. Air is much, much less dense than water, bringing the overall density of the mammoth down and making it more buoyant (able to float).

Forces in fluids
Two forces act on an object in water: the weight of the object and a force called upthrust. When you put an object in water, it pushes some of the water out of the way. The water pushes upward with a force equal to the weight of water displaced. This is upthrust. If the object is denser than water, its weight will be greater than the upthrust and it will sink. If its density is less than water, the upthrust will be greater and it will float.

Ship's hull contains air, lowering its density

Weight

A heavy concrete block weighs more than the amount of water it displaces

Weight

Upthrust

The ship displaces more water, producing more upthrust

Upthrust

Floating

Would a mammoth sink or swim? That depends on whether it has taken swimming lessons. But whether or not the mammoth floats depends on its density—the amount of matter packed into it. Objects that are less dense than water will float, while those that are more dense will sink.

Changing density

Mammoths are mammals, and mammals float. That's because their bodies are slightly less dense than water. A mammoth in water would probably bob with its head above and its body submerged in the water. By donning a rubber ring or a weight belt, the mammoth can rise above the surface or sink to the bottom.

Sinking

This mammoth is wearing a heavy diving suit and a belt of weights. The combined density of the mammoth and its outfit is now much greater than the density of water, so the mammoth can have a stroll on the seabed.

Weight belt
These small weights are made of very dense metal.

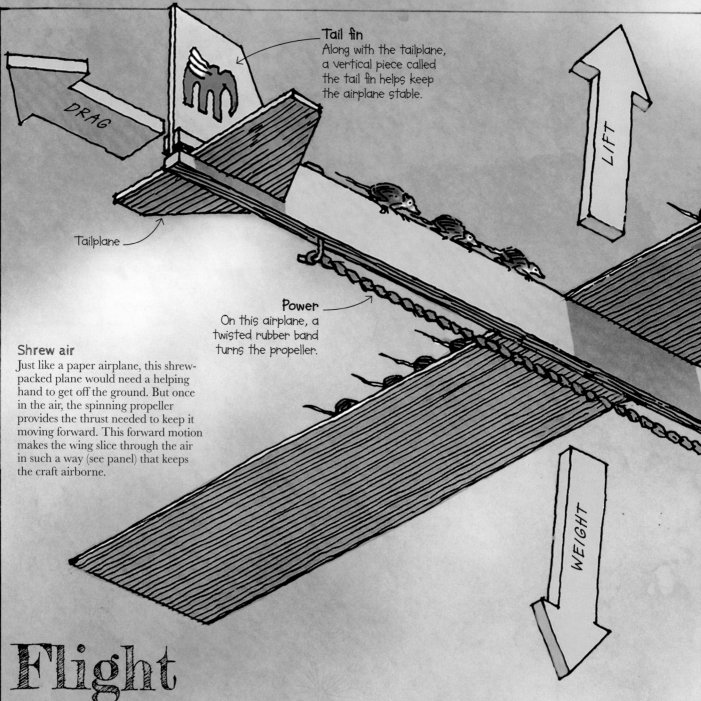

Tail fin
Along with the tailplane, a vertical piece called the tail fin helps keep the airplane stable.

DRAG

LIFT

Tailplane

Power
On this airplane, a twisted rubber band turns the propeller.

Shrew air
Just like a paper airplane, this shrew-packed plane would need a helping hand to get off the ground. But once in the air, the spinning propeller provides the thrust needed to keep it moving forward. This forward motion makes the wing slice through the air in such a way (see panel) that keeps the craft airborne.

WEIGHT

Flight

Anything that flies—whether it's a jumbo jet or a paper airplane—has the same four forces acting on it. Lift is the force that keeps the aircraft aloft, while the craft's weight pulls it down. Thrust is the force that pushes the aircraft forward, while drag, or air resistance, pulls it back. To take off, thrust and lift must be greater than drag and weight. Once in the air, if the forces are balanced the aircraft will fly straight ahead at a steady speed.

Fearless fliers
Is it a bird? Is it a plane? It's some fearless elephant shrews in a flying machine! Their balsa-wood flier is powered by a simple rubber band: hand-turning the propeller twists the rubber band until it can't twist any more. When you let the propeller go, the rubber band untwists, spinning the propeller rapidly and pushing the plane forward.

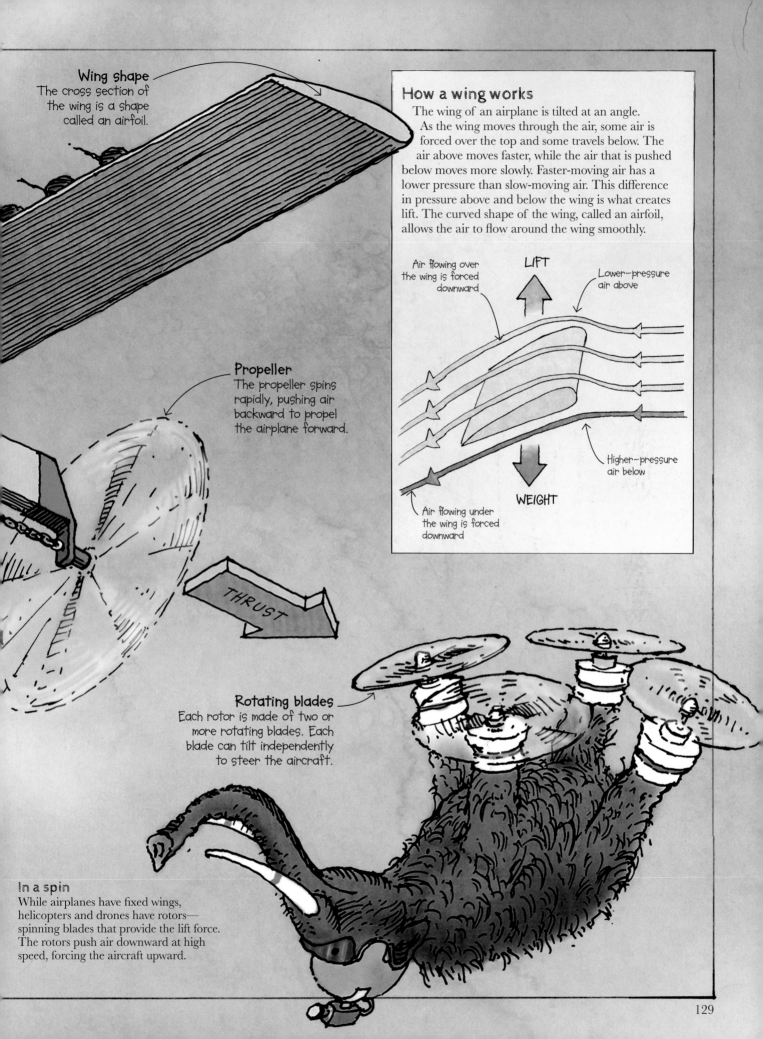

Wing shape
The cross section of the wing is a shape called an airfoil.

How a wing works

The wing of an airplane is tilted at an angle. As the wing moves through the air, some air is forced over the top and some travels below. The air above moves faster, while the air that is pushed below moves more slowly. Faster-moving air has a lower pressure than slow-moving air. This difference in pressure above and below the wing is what creates lift. The curved shape of the wing, called an airfoil, allows the air to flow around the wing smoothly.

Air flowing over the wing is forced downward

LIFT

Lower-pressure air above

Higher-pressure air below

WEIGHT

Air flowing under the wing is forced downward

Propeller
The propeller spins rapidly, pushing air backward to propel the airplane forward.

THRUST

Rotating blades
Each rotor is made of two or more rotating blades. Each blade can tilt independently to steer the aircraft.

In a spin
While airplanes have fixed wings, helicopters and drones have rotors—spinning blades that provide the lift force. The rotors push air downward at high speed, forcing the aircraft upward.

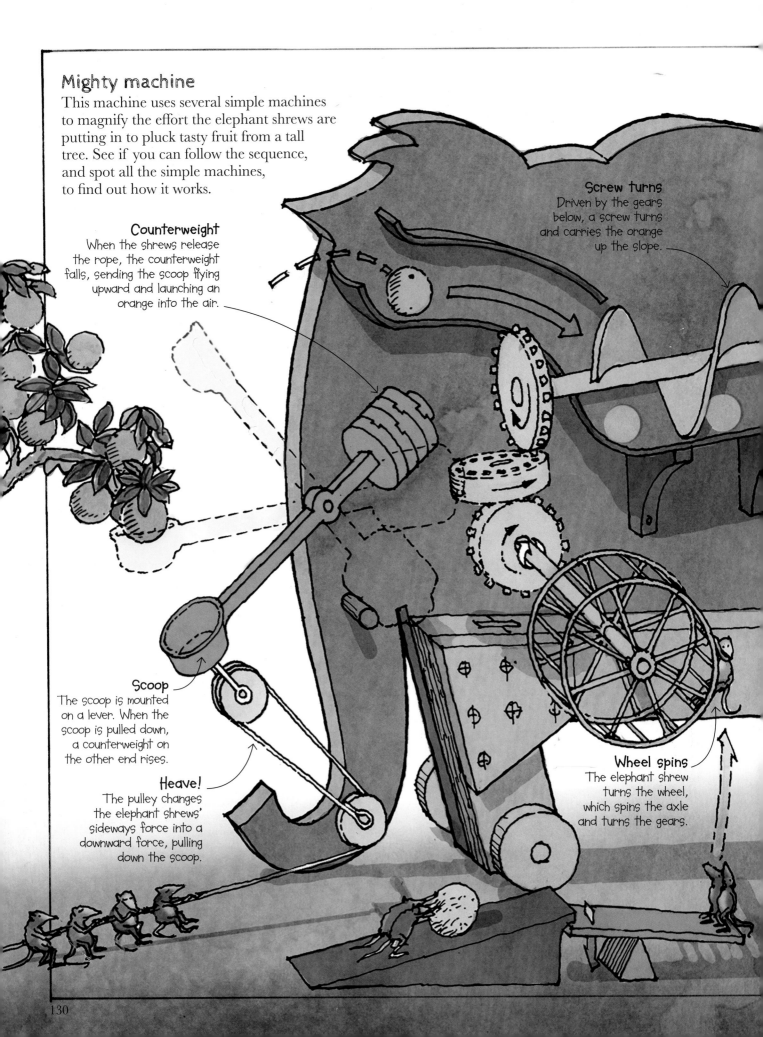

Mighty machine

This machine uses several simple machines to magnify the effort the elephant shrews are putting in to pluck tasty fruit from a tall tree. See if you can follow the sequence, and spot all the simple machines, to find out how it works.

Counterweight
When the shrews release the rope, the counterweight falls, sending the scoop flying upward and launching an orange into the air.

Screw turns
Driven by the gears below, a screw turns and carries the orange up the slope.

Scoop
The scoop is mounted on a lever. When the scoop is pulled down, a counterweight on the other end rises.

Heave!
The pulley changes the elephant shrews' sideways force into a downward force, pulling down the scoop.

Wheel spins
The elephant shrew turns the wheel, which spins the axle and turns the gears.

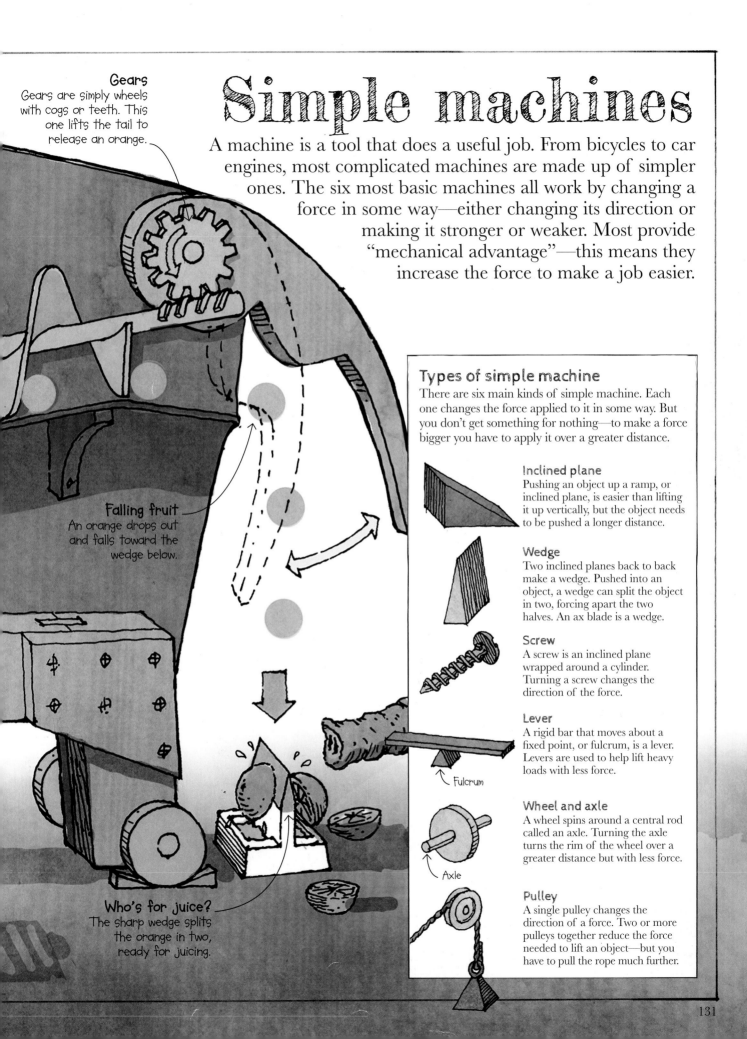

Gears
Gears are simply wheels with cogs or teeth. This one lifts the tail to release an orange.

Simple machines

A machine is a tool that does a useful job. From bicycles to car engines, most complicated machines are made up of simpler ones. The six most basic machines all work by changing a force in some way—either changing its direction or making it stronger or weaker. Most provide "mechanical advantage"—this means they increase the force to make a job easier.

Falling fruit
An orange drops out and falls toward the wedge below.

Who's for juice?
The sharp wedge splits the orange in two, ready for juicing.

Types of simple machine
There are six main kinds of simple machine. Each one changes the force applied to it in some way. But you don't get something for nothing—to make a force bigger you have to apply it over a greater distance.

Inclined plane
Pushing an object up a ramp, or inclined plane, is easier than lifting it up vertically, but the object needs to be pushed a longer distance.

Wedge
Two inclined planes back to back make a wedge. Pushed into an object, a wedge can split the object in two, forcing apart the two halves. An ax blade is a wedge.

Screw
A screw is an inclined plane wrapped around a cylinder. Turning a screw changes the direction of the force.

Lever
A rigid bar that moves about a fixed point, or fulcrum, is a lever. Levers are used to help lift heavy loads with less force.

Fulcrum

Wheel and axle
A wheel spins around a central rod called an axle. Turning the axle turns the rim of the wheel over a greater distance but with less force.

Axle

Pulley
A single pulley changes the direction of a force. Two or more pulleys together reduce the force needed to lift an object—but you have to pull the rope much further.

Earth and space

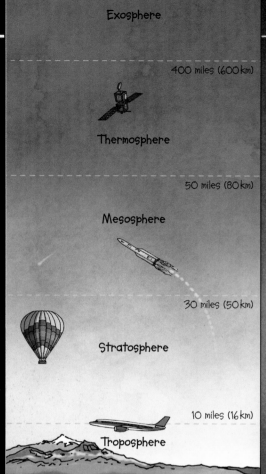

Exosphere

400 miles (600 km)

Thermosphere

50 miles (80 km)

Mesosphere

30 miles (50 km)

Stratosphere

10 miles (16 km)

Troposphere

Earth's atmosphere

The atmosphere is mainly oxygen and nitrogen, with small amounts of carbon dioxide and other gases. About 75 percent of it is concentrated in the lowest layer, the troposphere, which is also where all weather happens. The higher you go, the less gas each layer contains, until eventually the atmosphere merges with space.

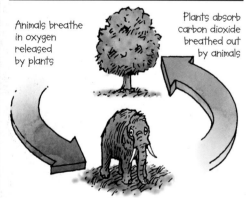

Animals breathe in oxygen released by plants

Plants absorb carbon dioxide breathed out by animals

Living planet

Life is everywhere on Earth—from the deepest ocean to the highest mountain peak. Most animals and plants need gases from the atmosphere to survive, and they release gases back into the atmosphere in a never-ending circle of life.

Earth

The ball of rock we call home is the third planet from the sun, and the only place in the whole universe we know for sure can support life. Nearly three-quarters of its rocky surface layer is covered by oceans of liquid water, and the whole planet is surrounded by an envelope of gases called the atmosphere. Inside, the planet is a churning ball of scorching rock and metal, which gets hotter the deeper you go.

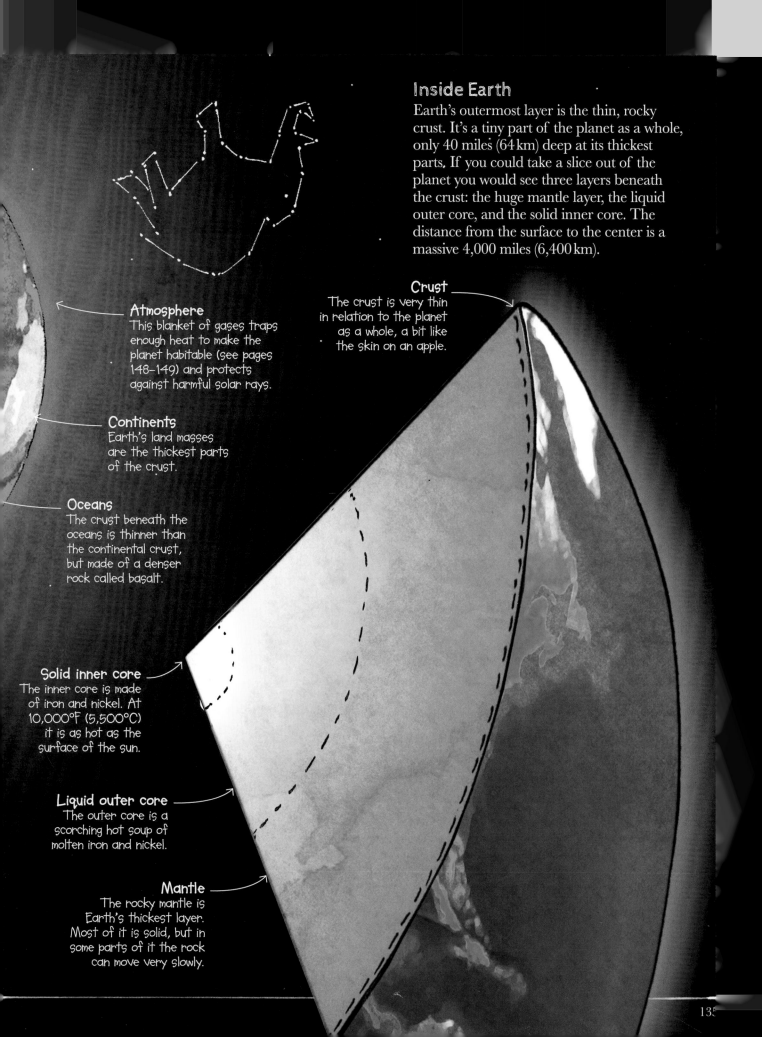

Inside Earth

Earth's outermost layer is the thin, rocky crust. It's a tiny part of the planet as a whole, only 40 miles (64 km) deep at its thickest parts. If you could take a slice out of the planet you would see three layers beneath the crust: the huge mantle layer, the liquid outer core, and the solid inner core. The distance from the surface to the center is a massive 4,000 miles (6,400 km).

Crust
The crust is very thin in relation to the planet as a whole, a bit like the skin on an apple.

Atmosphere
This blanket of gases traps enough heat to make the planet habitable (see pages 148–149) and protects against harmful solar rays.

Continents
Earth's land masses are the thickest parts of the crust.

Oceans
The crust beneath the oceans is thinner than the continental crust, but made of a denser rock called basalt.

Solid inner core
The inner core is made of iron and nickel. At 10,000°F (5,500°C) it is as hot as the surface of the sun.

Liquid outer core
The outer core is a scorching hot soup of molten iron and nickel.

Mantle
The rocky mantle is Earth's thickest layer. Most of it is solid, but in some parts of it the rock can move very slowly.

Pacific plate
The largest tectonic plate lies under the Pacific Ocean.

Plate boundary
The places where two plates meet are called plate boundaries.

Under the crust
Below the thin crust is the hot mantle layer.

Earth's puzzle pieces

The tectonic plates fit snugly together just like a gigantic jigsaw puzzle. The plates are moving very slowly, carrying Earth's landmasses with them. This means that millions of years ago the continents looked very different from the way they do today.

Moving mantle

The tectonic plates move because they sit on top of Earth's mantle, which is made from rock so hot that it is semi-molten and can move. The rock moves in currents that circulate the heat (see page 83)—the hottest rock rises, then cools, and sinks. As the mantle rock nearest the surface moves in this cycle it carries the crust along with it.

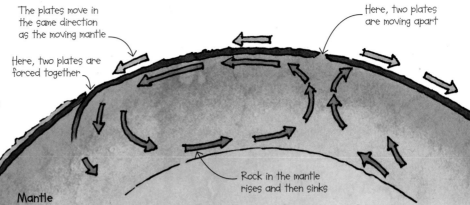

The plates move in the same direction as the moving mantle

Here, two plates are forced together

Here, two plates are moving apart

Rock in the mantle rises and then sinks

Crust

Mantle

Plate tectonics

Earth's surface layer is always on the move. It is made up of lots of fragments called tectonic plates that fit together like huge puzzle pieces and float on top of the mantle layer below. The plates move incredibly slowly, about as fast as your fingernails grow, but where they meet huge forces can be unleashed, causing dramatic changes to the landscape.

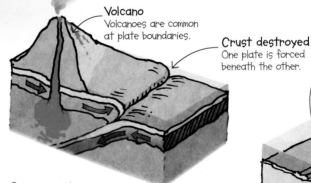

Volcano
Volcanoes are common at plate boundaries.

Crust destroyed
One plate is forced beneath the other.

New crust forms
Magma rises and cools to form new crust.

Transform
A transform boundary is where two plates are sliding past each other. The line between the two plates is called a fault. Earthquakes are common at transform boundaries, as the plates grind against each other.

Convergent
Plates collide at convergent boundaries. Crust is destroyed as one plate sinks under the other. Mountain ranges may be pushed up as the upper plate crumples.

Plate boundaries

At the boundaries where two or more tectonic plates meet, colossal forces are at work. New crust is created and old crust destroyed; mountain ranges rise; and huge cracks, or rifts, appear. There are three main types of plate boundary, depending on whether the plates are moving together, apart, or past each other.

Divergent
Where plates are pulling apart, molten magma from the mantle rises to fill the gap, forming new crust. This forms rift valleys and mid-ocean ridges.

Making rocks

Rocks are formed incredibly slowly, over many thousands of years, as the movement of Earth's tectonic plates heats and squeezes rocks underground, and wind and water wear down surface rocks and carry the sediments away. The mammoths are attempting to recreate these conditions in their kitchen laboratory.

Hot rocks

You need immense heat to melt rocks—the mammoth's saucepan isn't going to cut it. But deep inside Earth, conditions are just right. Melted rock is called magma. When magma cools and solidifies it forms igneous rock. Granite and basalt are igneous rocks. Igneous rocks are hard.

Cooling

The speed at which the rock cools down affects what it will look like. Igneous rocks that cool slowly contain large, visible crystals.

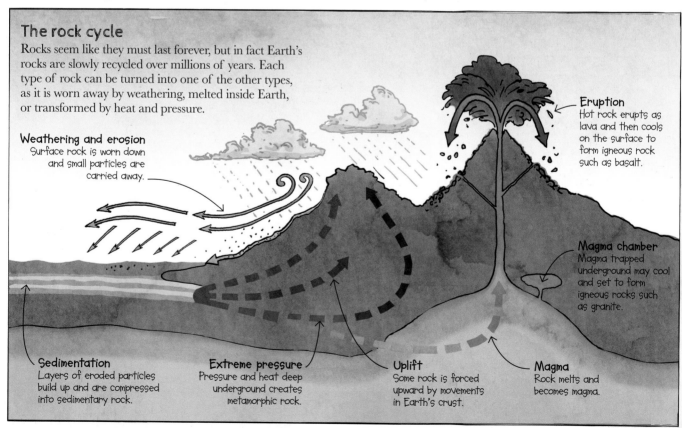

The rock cycle

Rocks seem like they must last forever, but in fact Earth's rocks are slowly recycled over millions of years. Each type of rock can be turned into one of the other types, as it is worn away by weathering, melted inside Earth, or transformed by heat and pressure.

Weathering and erosion
Surface rock is worn down and small particles are carried away.

Eruption
Hot rock erupts as lava and then cools on the surface to form igneous rock such as basalt.

Magma chamber
Magma trapped underground may cool and set to form igneous rocks such as granite.

Sedimentation
Layers of eroded particles build up and are compressed into sedimentary rock.

Extreme pressure
Pressure and heat deep underground creates metamorphic rock.

Uplift
Some rock is forced upward by movements in Earth's crust.

Magma
Rock melts and becomes magma.

Rocks

The rocks that form Earth's crust are made from naturally occurring substances called minerals. These are chemical compounds that form solid crystals and come together in different combinations to make rock. There are three main types of rock: igneous, metamorphic, and sedimentary. Each is formed in a different way, giving each type its own distinctive characteristics.

Pressure cooker
Sadly for the mammoth, this pressure cooker will never reach the kind of pressure needed to make metamorphic rock.

Under pressure
Making metamorphic rock requires intense pressure and heat. As rocks underground are crushed by tectonic forces or exposed to hot magma they are transformed without being melted. Marble is a metamorphic rock that forms from the sedimentary rock limestone. Most metamorphic rocks are hard and many have colored stripes made of different minerals.

Squashed sediments
Sedimentary rocks are made from ground-up pieces of rock or animal remains such as shell fragments. These sediments build up over time so the bottom layers get squashed together under pressure, turning to rock. Sedimentary rocks, such as chalk, are usually quite soft and crumbly.

Layers
Sedimentary rock often contains distinct layers of different colors.

How fossils form

The formation of a fossil takes many millions of years. Most fossils we have now are skeletons or shells that have been turned to stone. This process happens when an animal dies in or near water, and is quickly covered by mud or sand before it can completely decompose or be eaten. Because water is essential to this process, many fossils are formed from sea creatures.

Watery death
A Tyrannosaurus rex drowns in a lake or swamp. Its body sinks to the bottom and the soft parts begin to decompose, leaving behind only the hard skeleton.

Sediment layers
Over time, the skeleton is covered in layers of soft sediment (mud and sand). These build up and over millions and millions of years are compressed to form solid rock.

A stone skeleton
As the skeleton is buried, minerals dissolved in the water enter pores in the bones and solidify. Gradually the bones turn to stone.

Exposed
After millions of years, movements of Earth's crust bring the rock with the fossil in it to the surface. As the wind or water wears away the rock, the fossil may finally be revealed.

Fossils

When a living thing dies it usually decomposes and vanishes forever. In very special circumstances, however, it can leave a record of itself that lasts for billions of years. We call these records fossils. They are very rare, but they help us understand the fantastic creatures that used to roam Earth.

Uncovering a fossil
Water can be used to loosen the sediment around a fossil.

Revealed
Fossils are exposed when the rock they are in is weathered away.

Sedimentary rock
Most fossils are found in soft sedimentary rock (see page 139).

Reading the soil
The soil around a fossil can indicate what the animal's environment was like when it was alive.

Tools
Paleontologists use hammers, trowels, and brushes to carefully clear away the rock and free a fossil.

Expert excavation

An ancient fossilized dinosaur skull is being uncovered by these careful critters. Fossils are very fragile, so paleontologists (people who study fossils) must be extra careful when digging them out. Most fossils form from the hard parts of an animal, such as its bones or teeth, but fossilized imprints of feathers, plants, and even footprints are also found.

Water cycle

The water on Earth is constantly moving between the sea, the air, and the land in a never-ending cycle. The amount of water stays the same, it just moves from place to place and changes form. This constant recycling of water means that when you take a drink from the tap it's the same stuff thirsty mammoths were drinking thousands of years ago.

Clouds
Water vapor cools as it rises and condenses into tiny liquid droplets that form clouds.

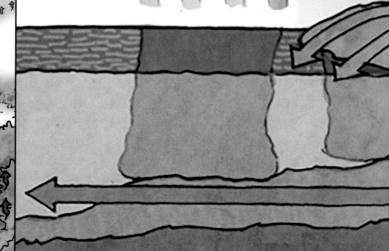

Water vapor
Heated by the sun, water turns to vapor and rises into the atmosphere.

Transpiration

Most of the water vapor in the atmosphere comes from evaporated sea water, but some also comes from plants. Plants take up water from the ground through their roots and release it through their leaves in a process called transpiration. Rainforests give off so much water vapor that they create low-hanging clouds.

Clouds
The water in the clouds will eventually fall as rain.

Trees release water vapor from their leaves into the air

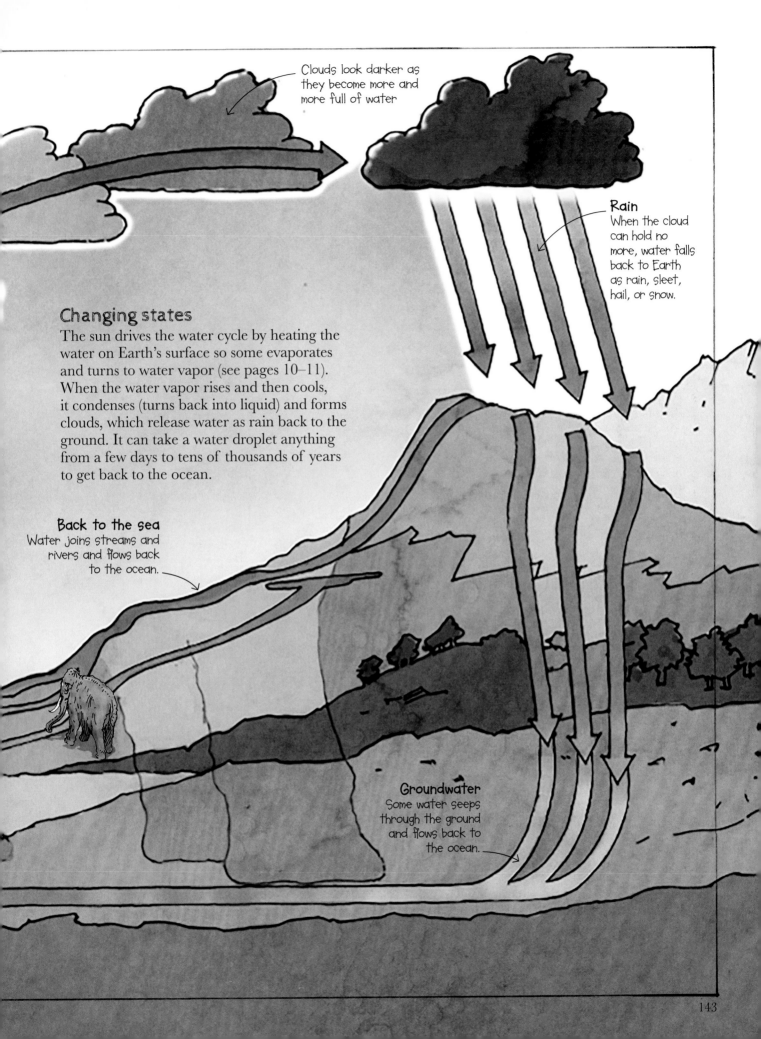

Clouds look darker as they become more and more full of water

Rain
When the cloud can hold no more, water falls back to Earth as rain, sleet, hail, or snow.

Changing states

The sun drives the water cycle by heating the water on Earth's surface so some evaporates and turns to water vapor (see pages 10–11). When the water vapor rises and then cools, it condenses (turns back into liquid) and forms clouds, which release water as rain back to the ground. It can take a water droplet anything from a few days to tens of thousands of years to get back to the ocean.

Back to the sea
Water joins streams and rivers and flows back to the ocean.

Groundwater
Some water seeps through the ground and flows back to the ocean.

Seasons

In many parts of the world, the year is split into distinct seasons: spring, summer, fall, and winter. In summer the days are longer and warmer, while winter days are short and cold. The reason for this is that Earth spins on a tilted axis. The axis is an imaginary line running through the planet from pole to pole. The tilt of the axis means that different parts of the globe tilt toward or away from the sun at different times of the year.

December

The southern hemisphere is now tilted toward the sun, bringing warmer temperatures and longer days. It is winter in the northern hemisphere, which is tilted away from the sun.

Direct light

When a hemisphere is tilted toward the sun it receives more direct sunlight. The sun is shining directly overhead so its light is more concentrated and feels hotter. You can demonstrate this with a flashlight and a ball. If you shine the flashlight directly onto the ball, the light is concentrated in one place. If you use the same flashlight to illuminate a larger area of the ball, the light spreads out and is weaker.

Direct light
The light is concentrated in one area.

Diffused light
The same amount of light spreads out over a larger area.

Tilted Earth

These mobile mammoths are demonstrating why the seasons happen using giant globe models. Each model is mounted on a pole that represents Earth's tilted axis. Because the planet is always tilted in the same direction, as it moves around the sun its hemispheres (northern and southern halves) tilt either toward or away from the sun.

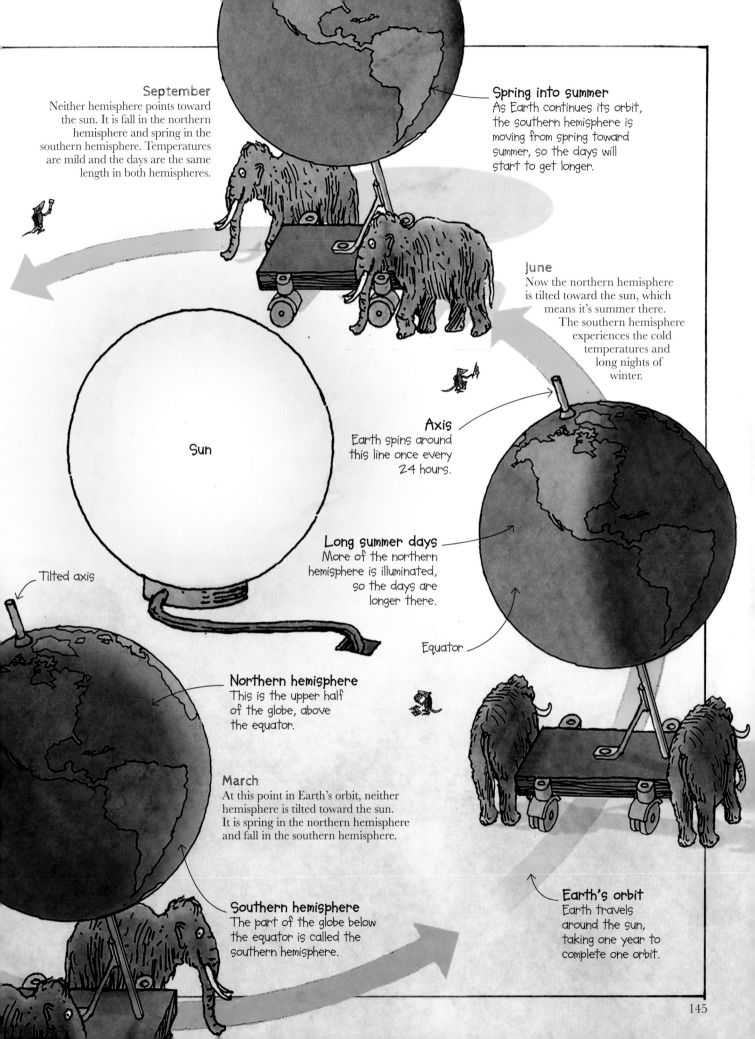

September
Neither hemisphere points toward the sun. It is fall in the northern hemisphere and spring in the southern hemisphere. Temperatures are mild and the days are the same length in both hemispheres.

Spring into summer
As Earth continues its orbit, the southern hemisphere is moving from spring toward summer, so the days will start to get longer.

June
Now the northern hemisphere is tilted toward the sun, which means it's summer there. The southern hemisphere experiences the cold temperatures and long nights of winter.

Sun

Axis
Earth spins around this line once every 24 hours.

Long summer days
More of the northern hemisphere is illuminated, so the days are longer there.

Equator

Tilted axis

Northern hemisphere
This is the upper half of the globe, above the equator.

March
At this point in Earth's orbit, neither hemisphere is tilted toward the sun. It is spring in the northern hemisphere and fall in the southern hemisphere.

Southern hemisphere
The part of the globe below the equator is called the southern hemisphere.

Earth's orbit
Earth travels around the sun, taking one year to complete one orbit.

Climate

The weather is what's going on in the air around us—whether it is rainy or dry, windy or still, sunny or overcast. The weather changes from day to day but the typical weather of a particular area is known as its climate. Lots of things can affect an area's climate, including its height above sea level, distance from the sea, and whether it is flat or mountainous. But the main factor is its distance from the equator.

Climate zones

The equator is an imaginary line around the center of Earth. This part of the globe receives the most direct sunlight, so it has a hot, sunny, tropical climate. The polar regions, far from the equator, receive the least direct sunlight and have cold, frosty climates. Next to the polar regions are the temperate zones, and between the temperate and tropical zones lie the subtropics.

Temperate zones

Earth's temperate zones have four distinct seasons—spring, summer, fall, and winter—each with different weather patterns. Summers are warm and winters are cold, with large temperature differences between the two. Some temperate regions are wet while others, such as the Mediterranean, are drier.

Tropical zones

The area around the equator is warm all year. Some tropical areas have lots of rain throughout the year, while others have a rainy season and a dry season. The combination of heat and plenty of rain means that dense tropical forests can grow in these areas, such as the Amazon rainforest.

Subtropical zones

The bands between the tropics and the temperate regions have hot, humid summers and mild, rainy winters, where temperatures rarely drop below freezing. However, some subtropical areas receive little to no rainfall all year. Many of the world's deserts are in these zones.

Polar zones

The regions around the poles are extremely cold and dry all year. Although many parts are covered with ice and snow, there is very little precipitation (rain or snowfall). The polar zones are harsh environments—though a woolly mammoth would feel right at home here.

Greenhouse effect

Just as a glass greenhouse keeps plants warm by trapping heat inside, gases in Earth's atmosphere stop warmth from the sun escaping back into space. Without this greenhouse effect, our planet would be too cold to support life as we know it.

Some energy is reflected by Earth's surface

Some energy is reflected back into space by the atmosphere

Sunlight
Energy from the sun enters the atmosphere, providing light and warmth.

Earth warms up
Energy from the sun warms Earth. The warm Earth gives off heat (infrared radiation).

Greenhouse gases

Earth's atmosphere is mainly nitrogen and oxygen, but it contains small amounts of greenhouse gases, such as carbon dioxide. These gases absorb heat and stop it from disappearing into space. Human activities are increasing the levels of these gases dramatically.

Farming
Intensive farming, especially of cattle, produces greenhouse gases.

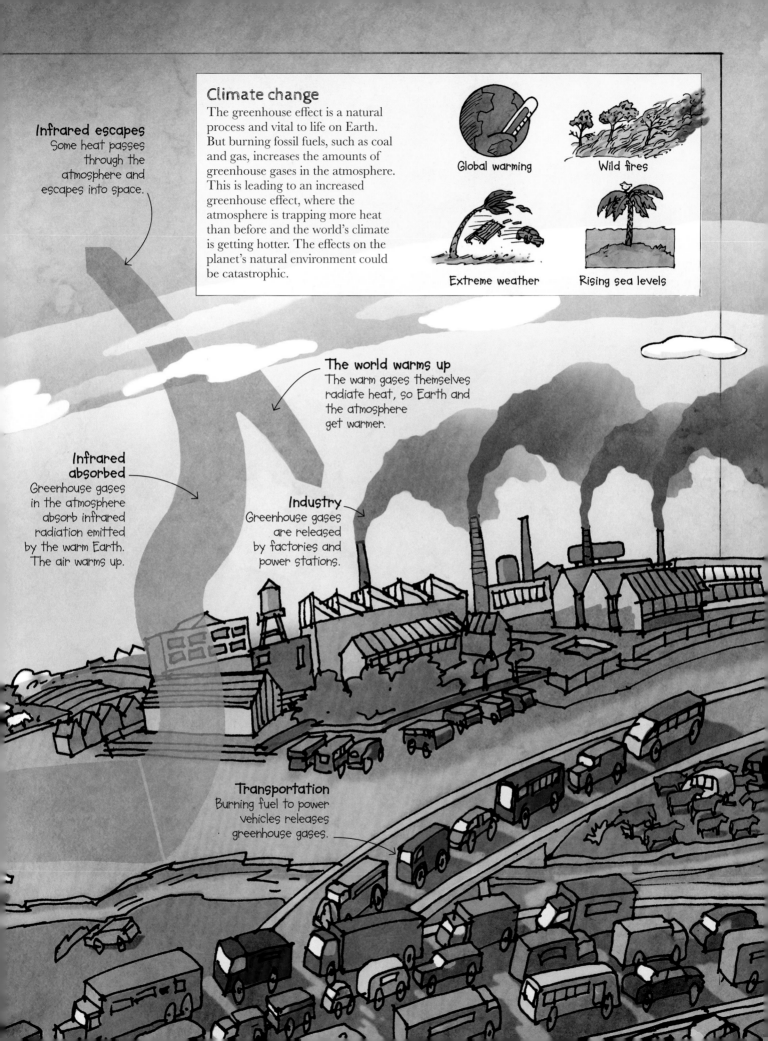

Climate change

The greenhouse effect is a natural process and vital to life on Earth. But burning fossil fuels, such as coal and gas, increases the amounts of greenhouse gases in the atmosphere. This is leading to an increased greenhouse effect, where the atmosphere is trapping more heat than before and the world's climate is getting hotter. The effects on the planet's natural environment could be catastrophic.

Global warming

Wild fires

Extreme weather

Rising sea levels

Infrared escapes
Some heat passes through the atmosphere and escapes into space.

The world warms up
The warm gases themselves radiate heat, so Earth and the atmosphere get warmer.

Infrared absorbed
Greenhouse gases in the atmosphere absorb infrared radiation emitted by the warm Earth. The air warms up.

Industry
Greenhouse gases are released by factories and power stations.

Transportation
Burning fuel to power vehicles releases greenhouse gases.

Moon

The moon is Earth's constant companion in space. It is close enough that many of its features can be seen with the naked eye. It shines brightly in the night sky, but it doesn't have any light of its own—the light we see is actually reflected from the sun. Unlike Earth, the moon is a dead world because it has no water or air to support life.

Mars-sized asteroid strikes Earth

Formation of the moon

The moon formed about 4.5 billion years ago. No one knows for sure, but the most common theory suggests that a Mars-sized asteroid collided with the newly formed Earth. Debris from the collision was flung into Earth's orbit, where it eventually clumped together into one large, rocky mass.

Moon suit
A real spacesuit would protect all parts of an astronaut's body.

On the surface

This four-legged space explorer has a close-up view of the moon's rocky, cratered surface. Most of the craters were formed billions of years ago, when asteroids smashed into the young moon. The biggest impacts made enormous craters that flooded with lava from inside the moon. The lava cooled and solidified, forming large, dark plains called maria, or seas.

Lunar movements

The moon orbits around Earth, but it also spins on its axis. One orbit around Earth takes the same amount of time as a full spin, so we always see the same side of the moon, called the near side. We also see different portions of the moon's sunlit surface during its orbit. We call these the phases of the moon.

New moon

Waxing crescent   **Waning crescent**

Phases of the moon
During its orbit, the moon seems to change shape. As it grows, it is said to be waxing, and as it shrinks, it is said to be waning. A gibbous moon is closer to full, while only a sliver is visible during a crescent moon. A full moon is when the entire near side is lit up by the sun. Only the far side is lit during the new moon.

First quarter   **Last quarter**

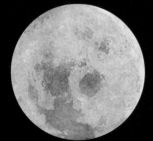

Waxing gibbous   **Waning gibbous**

Full moon

Near side
This side always faces Earth. It has more maria and fewer craters than the far side.

Far side
This unfamiliar view of the moon has many more craters than the near side.

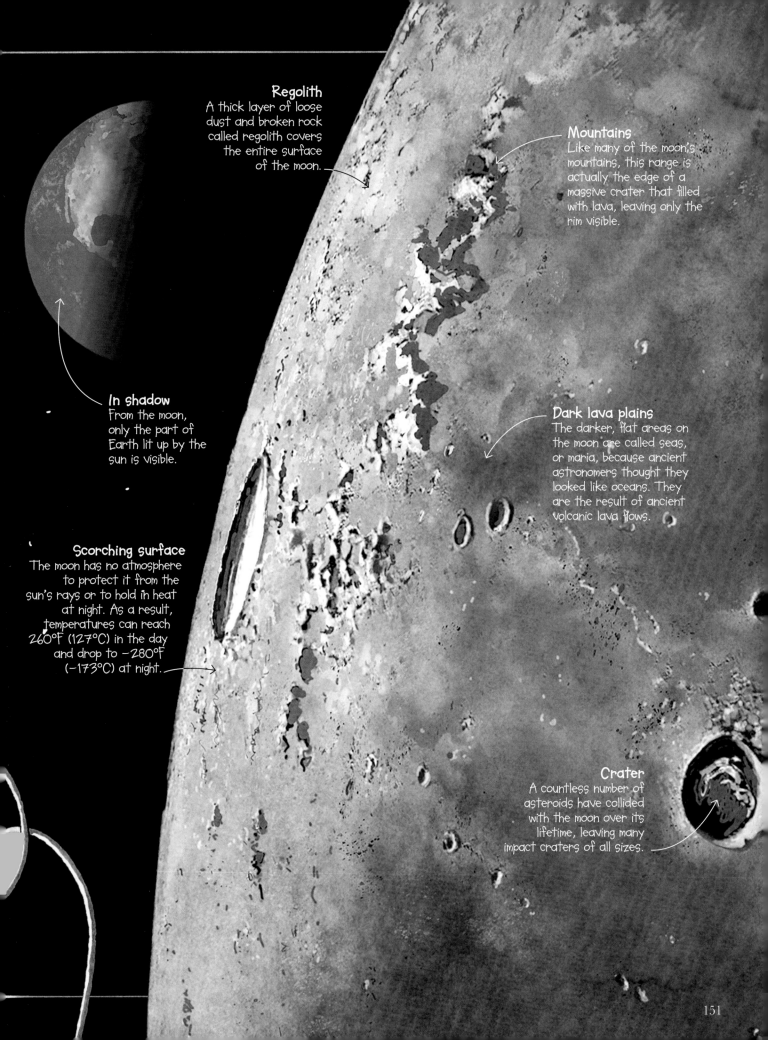

Regolith
A thick layer of loose dust and broken rock called regolith covers the entire surface of the moon.

Mountains
Like many of the moon's mountains, this range is actually the edge of a massive crater that filled with lava, leaving only the rim visible.

In shadow
From the moon, only the part of Earth lit up by the sun is visible.

Dark lava plains
The darker, flat areas on the moon are called seas, or maria, because ancient astronomers thought they looked like oceans. They are the result of ancient volcanic lava flows.

Scorching surface
The moon has no atmosphere to protect it from the sun's rays or to hold in heat at night. As a result, temperatures can reach 260°F (127°C) in the day and drop to −280°F (−173°C) at night.

Crater
A countless number of asteroids have collided with the moon over its lifetime, leaving many impact craters of all sizes.

Solar system

The solar system is Earth's gigantic neighborhood in space. At the center is the sun, the star whose enormous gravitational pull keeps the whole system together. Eight planets are held in orbit, along with billions of smaller objects, including asteroids, dwarf planets, and comets. This mammoth model shows the main members, but it's not to scale, or it would never fit on the page!

The planets

The four planets closest to the sun—Mercury, Venus, Earth, and Mars—are small, rocky worlds. The four outermost planets are gas giants, made mainly of hydrogen and helium.

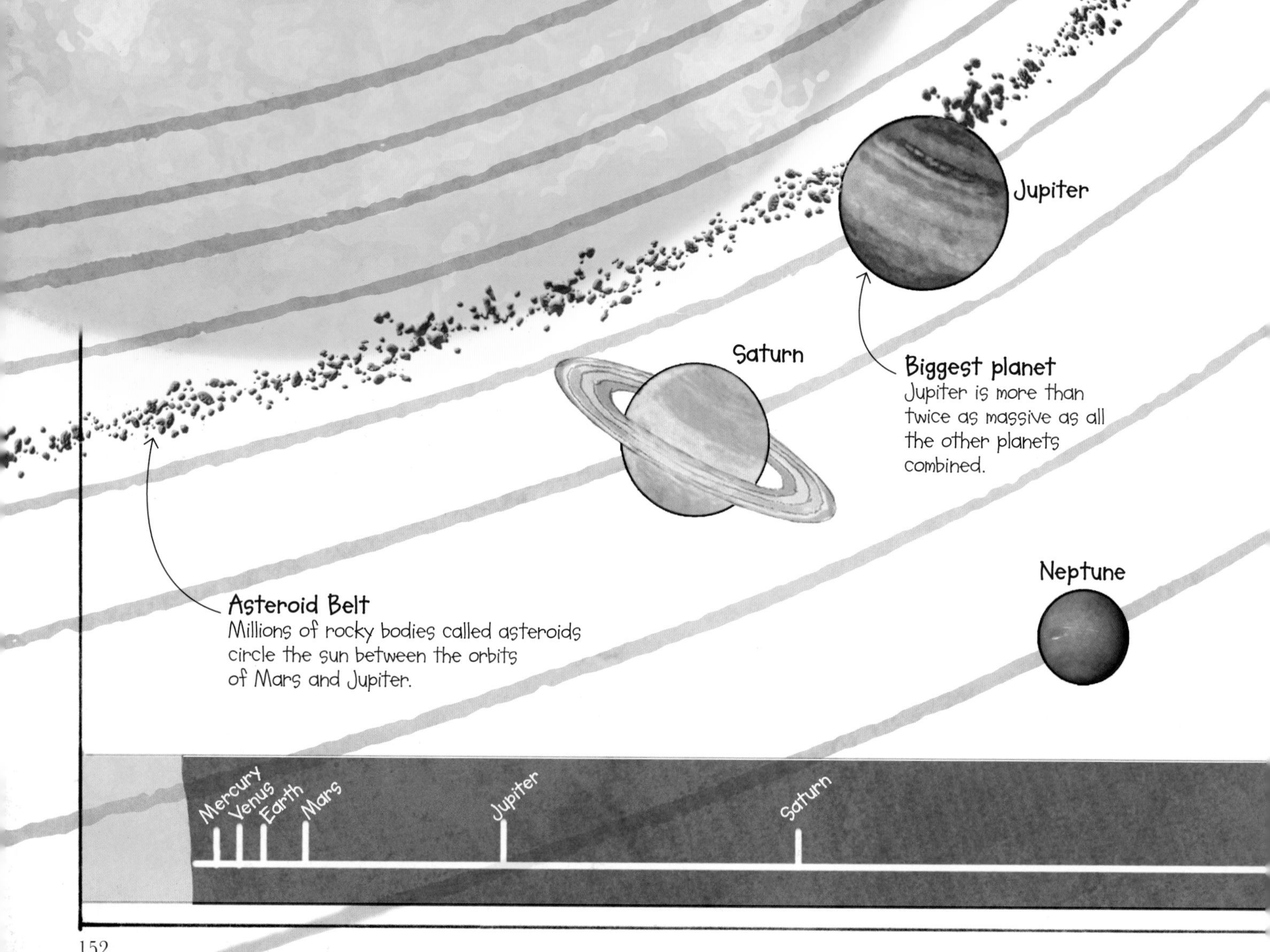

Mercury

Venus

Earth

Sun
This brilliantly hot ball of gas is so big that more than 1 million Earths could fit inside it.

Mars

Jupiter

Saturn

Biggest planet
Jupiter is more than twice as massive as all the other planets combined.

Neptune

Asteroid Belt
Millions of rocky bodies called asteroids circle the sun between the orbits of Mars and Jupiter.

Mercury Venus Earth Mars Jupiter Saturn

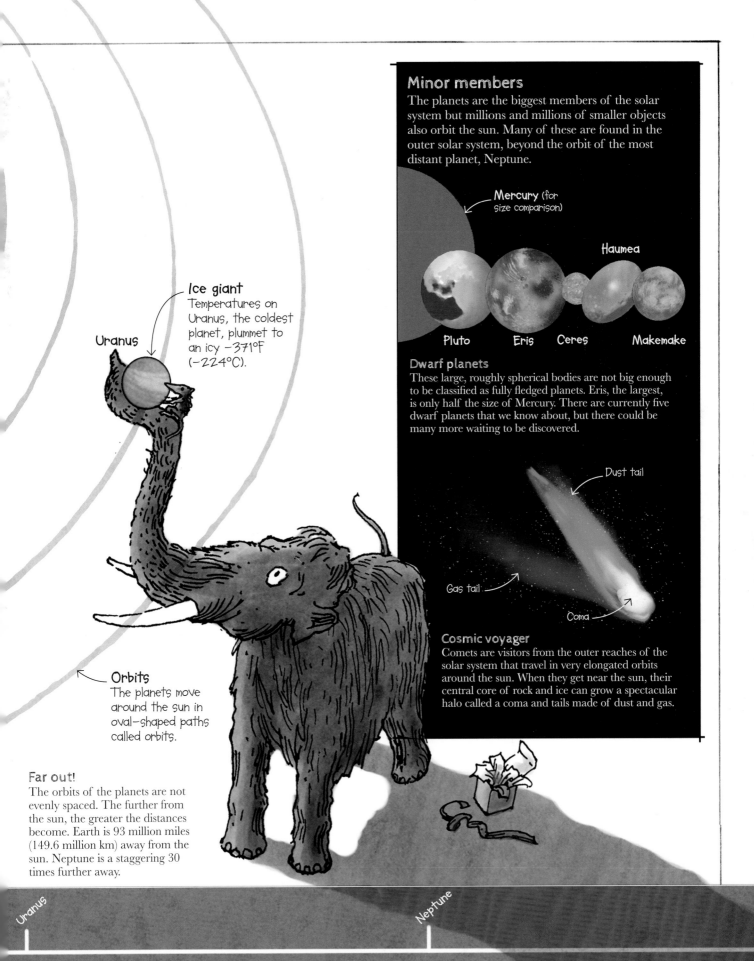

Minor members

The planets are the biggest members of the solar system but millions and millions of smaller objects also orbit the sun. Many of these are found in the outer solar system, beyond the orbit of the most distant planet, Neptune.

Mercury (for size comparison)

Haumea

Pluto   Eris   Ceres   Makemake

Dwarf planets

These large, roughly spherical bodies are not big enough to be classified as fully fledged planets. Eris, the largest, is only half the size of Mercury. There are currently five dwarf planets that we know about, but there could be many more waiting to be discovered.

Dust tail

Gas tail

Coma

Cosmic voyager

Comets are visitors from the outer reaches of the solar system that travel in very elongated orbits around the sun. When they get near the sun, their central core of rock and ice can grow a spectacular halo called a coma and tails made of dust and gas.

Ice giant

Temperatures on Uranus, the coldest planet, plummet to an icy −371°F (−224°C).

Uranus

Orbits

The planets move around the sun in oval-shaped paths called orbits.

Far out!

The orbits of the planets are not evenly spaced. The further from the sun, the greater the distances become. Earth is 93 million miles (149.6 million km) away from the sun. Neptune is a staggering 30 times further away.

Uranus

Neptune

153

Galaxies

A galaxy is a collection of stars, gas, and dust held together by gravity. Galaxies come in a variety of shapes and sizes, but they can be grouped into four main types: spiral, barred spiral, elliptical, and irregular. Scientists think there are hundreds of billions of galaxies in the universe.

Galaxy center has a long, flat shape

Spiral   Barred spiral

Elliptical   Irregular

Black hole

Scientists think most galaxies have a supermassive black hole at their centre. A black hole is the result of vast quantities of matter crushed into a point smaller than an atom. Its gravity is so strong that anything that passes too close is pulled in, even light.

Milky Way

Our solar system can be found in a galaxy called the Milky Way. All of the stars we can see in Earth's night sky are in the Milky Way. From our view inside the galaxy, we can never see its overall shape. But if we could see it from the same view as this furry space traveler, it would look like a giant, glowing whirlpool.

Arms spiral out from the center

Spinning in space

The Milky Way is a barred spiral galaxy with four arms that contain billions and billions of stars and large clouds of gas and dust. Everything in the Milky Way orbits around a massive black hole at its center, so the galaxy is constantly rotating in space. The Milky Way is so big that our solar system takes 240 million years to make one full orbit, and it would take millions of years to travel from one end of the galaxy to the other.

Galaxy arms
Each spiral arm contains billions of stars, huge clouds of gas and dust, and vast amounts of empty space.

You are here
Our solar system is on the Orion Arm, halfway between the galaxy's center and its outer edge.

Finding Andromeda
This pioneering pachyderm is off to see Andromeda, the Milky Way's neighboring galaxy.

Glossary

ANCESTOR
An animal or plant from which a more recent animal or plant is descended.

ANTIBODIES
Chemicals produced by the immune system that locate and mark bacteria and viruses for destruction.

ASTEROID
A space rock.

ATMOSPHERE
The layers of gas around a planet.

ATOM
The smallest unit of an element, containing protons, neutrons, and electrons.

AXIS
The invisible line around which Earth spins.

BACTERIA
Microscopic organisms with a simple, single-celled form. Some can cause disease.

CAPILLARIES
The smallest blood vessels in the body. Capillaries carry blood to and from the cells.

CARDIAC
Of or relating to the heart.

CELL
The smallest unit that forms a living organism.

CHLOROPHYLL
Green pigment plants use to trap energy from sunlight.

CHLOROPLAST
A tiny structure in a plant cell that contains chlorophyll and carries out photosynthesis.

CHROMOSOME
Threadlike structure that contains DNA, located in a cell's nucleus.

COMPOUND
A chemical substance made from atoms of two or more different elements.

CONCAVE
Describes an object that curves inward.

CONDENSATION
When a gas turns into a liquid.

CONDUCTION
The transfer of heat or electricity between solid objects.

CONDUCTOR
A material, such as metal, through which heat or electricity can easily flow.

CONSUMER
An animal that eats plants or other animals.

CONVECTION
The transfer of heat through a liquid or gas.

CONVEX
Describes an object that bulges in the center.

DECOMPOSER
An organism that breaks down decaying matter into nutrients.

DENSITY
The mass in a given volume of a substance.

DIGESTION
The process of breaking down food so the body can absorb nutrients.

DISPLACEMENT
When an object is placed in a fluid, the fluid is pushed aside to make room. The amount of displaced fluid equals the volume of the object.

DNA
A molecule that contains the instructions for life, found in the cells of living things.

DRAG
A force that acts to slow down objects moving through liquids or gases.

EGG CELL
Female sex cell.

ELECTRICITY
A way in which energy is transferred by a flow of charged particles.

ELECTROMAGNETIC SPECTRUM
The range of wavelengths and frequencies of electromagnetic radiation.

ELECTRON
A tiny, negatively charged particle found in an atom.

ELEMENT
A pure substance that can't be broken down any further.

ELEPHANT SHREW
A small, rodent-like mammal with a long snout. Also known as a sengi.

ENERGY
Energy is transferred every time something happens. It can be stored and transferred in different ways.

EQUATOR
The imaginary line around Earth's middle.

EROSION
The carrying away of weathered rock and sediment by wind, water, and ice.

EVAPORATION
When a liquid turns into a gas.

EVOLUTION
The way in which living things change from one generation to the next, brought about by natural selection.

EXCRETION
The body's process of removing waste products from living cells.

FERTILIZATION
When male and female sex cells join together to form a fertilized egg.

FLOWER
The reproductive part of a plant.

FLUID
A liquid or gas.

FORCE
A push or pull that acts on an object.

FRICTION
A force caused by two objects that rub against each other.

GAS
A state of matter in which particles spread out to fill a container.

GERMINATION
When a seed starts to sprout and grow into a plant.

GRAVITY
The force of attraction between two objects.

GREENHOUSE GASES
Gases in the atmosphere, such as carbon dioxide and methane, that absorb heat from the sun.

IMMUNITY
The body's ability to prevent illness from certain bacteria or viruses.

INFRARED
Radiation with wavelengths longer than visible light, which we feel as heat.

INSULATOR
A material, such as plastic, through which heat or electricity cannot easily flow.

LIGHT
The only part of the electromagnetic spectrum that we can see. Waves of different colored light make up the visible spectrum.

LIQUID
A state of matter in which the particles are loosely packed and easily slide past each other. Liquids flow, and take the shape of their container.

MAGMA
Molten rock deep within Earth.

MAMMAL
A warm-blooded animal that produces milk to feed its young.

MAMMOTH
A prehistoric mammal species that went extinct about 4,000 years ago. It is a close relative of the Asian elephant.

MASS
The amount of matter in an object.

MATTER
The "stuff" that makes up everything in the universe.

MICROSCOPE
An instrument that magnifies things that are too small to see with the naked eye.

MIXTURE
A combination of more than one substance or material.

MOLECULE
Two or more atoms that are bonded together.

NATURAL SELECTION
The process by which organisms with less successful traits die out, while organisms with more successful traits survive and are able to pass on their genes.

NECTAR
A sugary solution produced by flowers to attract pollinating animals.

NEURON
A nerve cell.

NEUTRON
A particle with no charge found within the nucleus of an atom.

NUCLEUS
The control center of a cell, where the cell's DNA is held. Also refers to the center of an atom, made of protons and neutrons.

NUTRIENT
Chemical substances that cells need to grow and repair.

ORBIT
The path that one object makes around another object due to gravity.

ORGANISM
A living thing.

PARTICLE
A very small piece of matter.

PHOTOSYNTHESIS
The chemical reaction used by organisms such as plants to make food, using carbon dioxide, water, and energy from sunlight.

POLLEN
Tiny grains produced by flowers, which contain the plant's male sex cells.

PRESSURE
The amount of force on a certain area, or the force caused by fluid particles hitting a surface.

PRODUCER
An organism that makes food through photosynthesis and is eaten by other animals.

PROTEIN
A substance that a living thing uses to form its tissues.

PROTON
A positively charged particle found in the nucleus of an atom.

RADIATION
Energy that travels through space in waves.

REFLECTION
When light bounces off an object and travels in a different direction.

REFRACTION
The bending of light as it travels from one substance to another.

RESPIRATION
The process by which living cells use oxygen to release energy from food.

SABER-TOOTHED CAT
A large, extinct cat species with long, curved upper canine teeth.

SEDIMENT
Small bits of weathered rock, minerals, and organic matter.

SEED
The part of a plant that contains the beginning of a new plant and enough food to help it grow.

SOLID
A state of matter in which the particles are tightly packed and can hold their own shape.

SPECIES
A group of living things that are similar to each other and can produce offspring.

SPERM CELL
Male sex cell. When a sperm fertilizes a female egg cell, the fertilized egg develops into a baby.

TECTONIC PLATE
A large piece of Earth's crust that floats on the mantle below.

UPTHRUST
An upward force exerted on an object in a fluid.

VELOCITY
The speed and direction of movement of an object.

VIRTUAL IMAGE
When looking in a mirrored surface or through a lens, an image formed due to the apparent source of light rays, versus their actual source.

VISIBLE SPECTRUM
See *Light*.

VOLUME
How much space an object takes up.

WATER VAPOR
Water in a gas state. Also called steam.

WAVELENGTH
The distance between two peaks in a wave.

WEATHERING
The wearing down of rock by wind, rain, or ice over a period of time.

Index

Page numbers in **bold** type refer to main entries